CHILD LANGUAGE

IN THE SAME SERIES

Series Editor: Richard Hudson

CHILD LANGUAGE

Second Edition

Jean Stilwell Peccei

London and New York

First published 1994

This edition first published 1999
by Routledge
11 New Fetter Lane, London EC4P 4EE

Simultaneously published in the USA and Canada
by Routledge
29 West 35th Street, New York. NY 10001

Reprinted 2000, 2001

Routledge is an imprint of the Taylor & Francis Group

© 1994, 1999 Jean Stilwell Peccei

Typeset in Times Ten by The Florence Group,
Stoodleigh, Devon

Printed and bound in Great Britain by TJ International Ltd,
Padstow, Cornwall

British Library Cataloguing in Publication Data
A catalogue record for this book is available from the British Library

Library of Congress Cataloguing in Publication Data
A catalogue record for this book is available from the Library of Congress

ISBN 0-415-19836-4

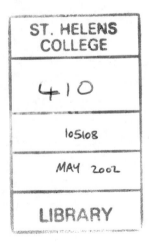

CONTENTS

This book is dedicated to my parents, Edward and Doris Stilwell.

USING THIS BOOK

This workbook has been written for all those who are embarking on the study of children's language for the first time and have little or no prior background in linguistics. Because of this, technical terminology has been kept to a minimum. Where specialist terms have been introduced, they are explained in the text. You will find them highlighted as KEY WORDS. You should not need to do any supplementary reading while you are working your way through this book. However, the **Further Reading** section at the end of the workbook will provide you with suggested background reading and the sources for the research and data which we will be discussing in the units.

Key word

Units 1–10 cover some of the basic techniques involved in studying children's acquisition of word meanings, sentence structure, word formation processes, conversation skills and pronunciation patterns. As you work through these units you will find a number of exercises. Some of these exercises involve the analysis of data from young children, while others are designed to give you the practical linguistic skills needed for this type of analysis. Each exercise is followed by a **Comment** section with a solution to the problem posed by the data and a further discussion of the topic under consideration. This workbook takes a 'hands on' approach to studying child language, and you will get much more out of the units if you complete each exercise before moving on to the **Comment** section.

At the end of each unit you will find **Further Exercises** which will give you the chance to practise and consolidate your skills. Answers to these exercises appear at the end of the workbook. The units also have **Supplementary Exercises** which allow for more independent work. These exercises do not have model answers and, if you are not using this book as part of a taught course, you may find it helpful to discuss your answers with someone else.

By the time you finish the first ten units, I hope that you will want to take your newly acquired skills into the real world and that you will want to learn even more about children's language development.

Unit 11 provides you with ideas and guidance for carrying out eighteen mini research projects. The projects (not all of which require access to a child) are designed to coincide with specific units and can be carried out by both individuals and groups. **Unit 12** gives an overview of some of the main issues involved in explaining language development and suggests other aspects of children's language which we have not been able to cover in this workbook but which are nevertheless fascinating areas of study.

ACKNOWLEDGEMENTS

I owe many thanks to the students who tested this workbook in its preliminary stages, to Professor Eve Clark who reviewed the first edition, to the teachers in other universities and colleges who have used this workbook with their students and provided suggestions for improvements to this new edition, and most of all to the series editor, Professor Richard Hudson, for his unfailingly patient and invariably helpful advice on writing for 'beginners' in linguistics. Their comments have proved invaluable, and any remaining mistakes and shortcomings are mine. I am grateful to Blackwell Publishers for permission to use the extracts from *A Child's Learning of English* by Paul Fletcher which appear in Corpus II and to Macmillan Publishing Company for permission to use the extracts from *Language Development and Language Disorders* by Lois Bloom and Margaret Lahey which appear in Corpora III and IV. And last but not least, I would like to thank two of my former students, Gayle Croker and Lucy Barker who provided the data for Corpora VI and VII.

STARTING TO TALK

1

> We introduce the study of language development and begin to analyse children's earliest vocabularies by the types of concepts which they first put into words.

Christian, one month old, not keen on having a bath:
   Waaaaaaa!

Christian, 2 years old, not keen on hearing a scary story:
   No talk!

Christian, 4½ years old, not keen on leaving for his
first day at school:
   Mum, I don't think I want to go through with this!

Christian's accomplishment was quite remarkable, if you think about it. Imagine yourself suddenly placed in a land where no one has ever heard English and whose inhabitants speak 'Yakish', a language both utterly unknown to you and not remotely similar to any language that you do know. Your task is to become a competent and confident speaker of Yakish. You must learn the correct form for making positive and negative statements, asking questions and making requests. You have to be able to describe people and things and talk about past, present and future events according to the rules of Yakish. In addition, you must be able to understand the meanings of at least 10,000 individual words in this language and be able to pronounce the words you use with a 'native accent'. Hearing Yakish and trying to speak it yourself are the only tools at your disposal. You cannot write anything down, use a tape-recorder, consult a book or hire a teacher. You have a little less than five years in which to do all this. If you want to, you can spend all your free time and energy on the task. Unlike the small child, you already know how to feed and dress yourself, and you do not have to bother with minor tasks like learning to walk or finding out how the world works while you are tackling the language.

Christian's accomplishment may have been remarkable, but it was certainly not unique. Children around the world, from all cultures and all language communities manage to become competent speakers of their native language in the first five years of life.

How children gain such a command of their native language with all its intricate systems of sound, meaning and grammatical structure in such a short space of time is a fascinating question. We cannot ask children how they are doing it. Nor can we remember how we did it ourselves. Much of the insight into the course of language development that we do have, has come from an analysis of the language that children actually produce. The purpose of this book is to give you some of the skills that are necessary for this kind of analysis.

As you will see, children do not passively soak up their native language. They actively apply themselves to cracking the code. In the process, they make mistakes. But these mistakes are not random ones. They reflect the rule systems that the children are building for themselves and provide an insight into the kinds of 'educated guesses' that they are making about the way their language works. Although we will be concentrating almost entirely on children acquiring English as their native language, the stages they go through and the strategies they use are similar in children everywhere.

By the time they are a year old, babies already seem to understand several words. They have also started to communicate with the people around them by their gestures and tone of voice. Then at about this age, children produce their first recognizable, meaningful words. They have started to communicate with **language**, and this is where we begin.

EXERCISE ✎

1.1 The words in the following list are typically among the first 50 or so words that children learn to say and use.

ball	allgone	no
dog	juice	Daddy
give	Mummy	milk
bye-bye	hi	car
dirty	nice	more
cat	yes	this
sit	up	down
baby	stop	put
go	shoe	biscuit

Not surprisingly, these words tend to be ones closely connected with the child's everyday world. But we can analyse this list in a bit more detail. Try classifying these words by the types of concepts which they express. For example:

1 Naming things or people (N): juice
2 Actions/events (A): give
3 Describing/modifying things (M): dirty
4 Personal/social words (S): bye-bye

In her study of eighteen children's first 50 words, Katherine Nelson (1973) classified the words in our list like this:

Comment

Naming things (N)	*Actions/events (A)*
ball	give
dog	put
juice	sit
Mummy	stop
Daddy	go
milk	up
cat	down
car	
baby	
shoe	
biscuit	

Personal/social (S)	*Modifying things (M)*
yes	dirty
hi	nice
no	more
bye-bye	this
	allgone

By classifying words in this way, Nelson was able to make some interesting observations. First, she noted that the largest group of words in her sample (about 60 per cent) were those that named people, animals and things. The second largest group were words that expressed or demanded actions. Usually, these were obvious actions like *sit* or *put*, but this group also included some location words like *up* and *down*. Young children usually use these words in the sense of *pick up* or *get down*. The next largest group was the MODIFIERS, like *mine*, *this* and *nice* which can be used to describe a range of people or objects. Personal/social words such as *yes*, *no* and *bye-bye* made up about 8 per cent of the sample overall.

Modifier

Nelson then looked more closely at the largest category of early words and analysed it by the kinds of things that tend to be named by children when they first start to speak.

EXERCISE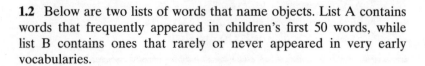

1.2 Below are two lists of words that name objects. List A contains words that frequently appeared in children's first 50 words, while list B contains ones that rarely or never appeared in very early vocabularies.

A	B
clock	sofa
key	floor
blanket	lamp
shoe	nappy
sock	pants
horse	house
car	tree
ball	park

What sorts of characteristics do the objects named in List A have which might account for them being among the first to be labelled by children?

Comment

Nelson found, as you have probably noticed, that the first objects named by children tend to be those which are small and easily handled by children. Notice that *shoe* and *sock* tend be acquired before *pants* or *nappy*. *Clock*, *key* and *blanket* are reasonably common while *lamp*, *floor* and *sofa* are not. Early words also tend to name things which move, make a noise, or change in some way . . . animals, vehicles and, of course, people. My elder son's first word was *ball*. His younger brother's was *Harvey* (his grandmother's cat). Large objects which simply **exist** in the child's world like trees and parks do not usually appear in children's very early vocabularies.

Up until now, we have been assuming that children's early words mean the same thing for them as they do for adults. In the next two units we will consider this question in greater detail. For now, here is some food for thought:

Child sucking a mint:
   There's a breeze in my mouth.

Child stomping on a spider:
   I can't die this spider!

Child picks up a shiny, crescent shaped leaf:
   Moon.

Child sees the postman:
   Daddy!

UNIT SUMMARY

Children's earliest words can be classified by meaning categories: object names, actions, modifiers, personal/social.

In children's first 50 spoken words, the largest meaning category is for object names.

The first objects named tend to be things that move or make a noise or which can be easily handled by the child.

🖉 **FURTHER EXERCISE**

1.3 Take your first look at the **Corpus of Child-Language Data** which we will be using throughout this book. For each underlined word in **Corpus I**, state the concept type as in **Exercise 1.1**. Note that these utterances are presented out of context. And, because children's early sentences tend to have words missing and usually lack word endings as well, some of the underlined words could have two possible meaning types. For example, in *Sound loud*: If the child were trying to say *The sound is loud*, then *sound* = N (name). If the child were trying to say *It sounds loud*, then *sound* = A (action/event). In these cases list both possible meaning types.

🖉 **SUPPLE-MENTARY EXERCISES**

1.4 By looking at **Corpus II:3–6** and **Corpus III:4–5**, you will be able to compare the speech of two children of the same age. What similarities and differences do you notice in their language?

1.5 Read through the entire **Corpus (I–VII)**, making some preliminary observations about children's language in terms of their pronunciation, the meanings they attach to words, the structure of their sentences, and the way that adults talk to young children. Then look at these excerpts from a children's novel written in 1916 in which we find 2-year-old Middy in conversation with her adult friend, Patty. Based on your reading of the corpus, how accurately has the author captured the language of a young child and the way that an adult might talk to her? (The author's narrative appears in brackets.)

1. P: Did the bad mans take you, baby?
   M: No. Muddy bing baby. Muddy DID bing Middy. An Muddy DID put Middy in au'mobile.
   P: Middy have au'mobile at home?

2. M: Middy ant dolly-baby.
   P: Very well, you shall have a dolly baby. This one or that one?
   M: No 'reat bid one. See? (She pointed to the largest doll of all.)
   An a dolly vadon. (This was translated to mean 'wagon' by the clerk who was more versed than Patty in baby language.)

3. P: Haven't you any father at all?
   M: Poor Middy dot no fader. No. No . . . Middy tay wiv Patty. Middy not go wiv bad nursie.

4. M: Me fink Patty booful! Me fink YOU'S booful! (This phrase was her highest praise . . . and as Mrs. Colton's arms closed around her . . .)

FINDING OUT WHAT WORDS MEAN

2

We look at how children learn new words and analyse early word meanings. We introduce the notions of overextension and under-extension as ways of characterizing the differences between the child's definition of a word and the adult definition.

Vocabulary development is one aspect of language acquisition that continues throughout our lives. For example, *nervine* is probably a word you have never encountered before. But if you look in the *Oxford English Dictionary*, you will find that it can mean either *soothing* or a *nerve tonic*. Of course, little children cannot take the easy way out and grab a dictionary. And yet, they add thousands of words to their vocabularies in the first five years of life.

✏ **EXERCISE**

2.1 Take a look at the way these 1–2-year-olds use the words *duck*, *white* and *ball*.

Child A: First uses *duck* upon seeing a duck swimming in a pond. Afterwards, he uses *duck* to refer to ducks in and out of water and to water with or without ducks swimming in it.

Child B: Uses *white* only to describe snow and is mystified when her father describes blank pages with the same word.

Child C: Uses *ball* to refer to balls, marbles, wheels and cement mixers!

In what ways do the children's meanings for *duck*, *white* and *ball* appear to differ from the generally accepted adult meanings for those words?

Comment

Child A has first associated the word *duck* with a situation in which both the duck and water were present, but has not yet realized that *duck* is a label for only one element of the situation.

Child B still has a very restricted use of the adjective *white* in thinking that it can only apply to snow. Actually, although she was mistaken in this case, such restrictions do occur in language. For example, although *blond* and *pale yellow* can refer to roughly the same colour, *blond* is generally restricted to describing hair.

Child C uses *ball* in a much wider sense than adults usually do. It seems to apply to several objects which share some but not all of a ball's characteristics – roundness and the ability to spin or roll.

These examples illustrate both the kinds of tasks facing children as they learn the words of their language and the kinds of initial guesses about word meanings that they make along the way.

When they hear words in a particular context, children first have to separate out which element of the situation is being symbolized by that particular string of sounds. When in doubt, children sometimes bundle several elements together under the same label as in the *duck* example. Another problem for children in the labelling task is to decide which particular string of sounds **is** the label. One afternoon Christian (age 18 months) pointed to a spider web and asked *What that*? His father replied *An abandoned spider web*. For several weeks Christian insisted on calling spider webs *bandons*.

Once children do reliably attach a label to a concept in a particular context, they then have to learn how far they should extend that label. For example, the child who first learns *cat* in relation to the family pet, must eventually learn that there are all sorts of furry meowing creatures in the world which can be called *cat*. She also has to learn that *cat* can apply to pictures of cats, toy cats, and statues of cats as well, in short, to the **concept** of *cat*. At first, children may assume a restricted use for a word which they have recently acquired, as did Child B with *white*. But eventually, by hearing other speakers apply the word in a variety of situations, they broaden out their own use of the word. This initial restriction of a word's use is sometimes called UNDEREXTENSION.

Underextension
Overextension

As we have seen with Child C, the OVEREXTENSION of words can also occur as children attempt to discover the limits to a word's application.

EXERCISE ✎

2.2 Look at these data from two different children. By looking at their overextensions, what sorts of guesses do these children appear to be making about the meaning of *cat*?

Language	First used for	Later used for
English	cats	dogs, sheep, cows, horses
Russian	cats	cotton, any soft material

The children in this example are trying to solve the problem of what **Comment**
cat means. They have to separate out the bundle of qualities that
allows them to label a particular object *cat* but does not allow them
to apply that label to dogs or pieces of soft cloth. Part of this process
involves hearing and learning new words such as *dog* or *cloth* which
help set limits to the applicability of the *cat* label. But children can
also **actively** apply themselves to solving the puzzle. In the process,
they sometimes focus on one or more qualities of the original object
named. In our data, the child learning English seems to be focusing
on general shape and perhaps movement. The Russian child, on the
other hand, seems to have focused on the soft texture of the fur.

Eve Clark (1973) made a study of parents' records of their children's early word use. These diary studies came from a number of
languages, but all reported instances of word overextension. By
looking at the overextensions, Clark concluded that while children
may differ in the particular qualities or features on which they base
their overextensions, they often choose physical ones like taste,
sound, movement, shape, size or texture. But this analysis does not
explain all types of overextensions.

✏ **EXERCISE**

2.3 Take a look at these data.

Language	Word	First used for	Later used for
French	*nenin*	mother's breast when asking to be fed	a button on a shirt, an eye in a picture, a bent elbow, asking for a square biscuit
English	*at*	a hat	scarf, ribbon, hairbrush

Can physical similarity alone account for the ways in which these children have extended *breast* and *hat*?

In the case of *breast*, the little boy does seem to be using a physical **Comment**
feature like shape in extending the word to buttons, eyes and elbows.
But in using *breast* to ask for a biscuit, he also appears to be using a
common function or use, providing food in this instance, to extend
the word to another object.

In the case of *hat*, again the child's overextensions are based not
on physical similarity but on a common function – something that
goes on the head, even if only momentarily as in the case of the
hairbrush.

EXERCISE ✎

2.4 Now, look at the way this child refers to three small round green objects. What pattern do you see underlying his choices?

Object	Child's word
Object	*Child's word*
pea	bean
wooden bead	ball
gooseberry	grape

Comment

A simple way to link the words in each pair is to say that they both belong to the same category. Peas and beans are vegetables. Wooden beads and balls are toys. Grapes and gooseberries are fruit. Children's overextensions are often a reflection of the way they are beginning to make sense of the world around them. By using their growing knowledge about the physical and functional similarities between the objects they encounter, children soon begin to put many of them into mental categories. From quite early on these categories can conform fairly closely to the way that adults divide up the world, although children may not yet be able to produce the names for the categories or the names for many of their individual members. Children's own efforts to explore and understand their physical environment are helped, of course, by their linguistic environment. The little boy in this example has probably heard adults ask him, *Would you like some fruit?* when offering either grapes or gooseberries. Adults may say to him *Eat up your vegetables*, regardless of whether he is spitting out his peas or throwing the baked beans on the floor. And *Let's pick up your toys* usually results in both the ball and the string of wooden beads ending up in the same basket.

As a final note, it is worth remembering that when analysing early word meanings from child data, it is not always easy to know what is going on inside children's heads when they use words in ways which differ from those of adults. It may not always be the case that they lack a reasonably clear idea of what the word means. There may be other explanations for a seemingly inappropriate use:

1 Children may know the correct word but find it difficult to pronounce. They may then choose a similar but more easily pronounceable word. One boy confidently showed his thumb when asked where it was, but used *finger* when speaking himself. He had particular trouble with the **th** sound and generally avoided words containing it.

2 Children may wish to comment on an object, but they may not know the correct word, or they may be momentarily unable to remember it. In that case, they may use a related word hoping that their listeners will make the connection and perhaps supply the appropriate word. The child who calls a guinea pig

cat may well know that it is not a cat but chooses the nearest label from the word stock currently available to her.

3 Children may have more complex propositions in their heads than evidenced by their single word 'remarks'. The child who says *biscuit* while pointing to the cupboard, is probably commenting on the biscuit's **location** rather than labelling the cupboard a *biscuit*.

In general, when analysing children's language, it is very important to have as much information as possible about the children themselves and about the situation in which they have used a particular word or group of words.

UNIT SUMMARY

Children's early word meanings sometimes differ from the adult meaning for the word.

Overextensions involve the child using the word more broadly than an adult would, while underextensions involve the child using the word more narrowly than an adult would.

Overextensions can reflect children's growing knowledge about the world as they start to notice similarities between objects and put them into mental categories.

✐ **FURTHER EXERCISES**

2.5 Rescorla (1980), who also studied children's overextensions, found it useful to divide them into three main types:

Categorical

CATEGORICAL: a word for one member of a clear category is extended to other members of that category. For example, a child uses *apple* to label other types of fruit.

Analogical

ANALOGICAL: a word for one object is extended to another object which is not in the same clear category but which still bears some similarity, either physical or functional, to the original object. For example, using *cat* for a soft scarf, or *hat* for a hairbrush.

Statement

STATEMENTS: these are almost like one-word sentences. Children are not labelling an object but making a statement about it in relation to another object. For example, saying *Dolly* upon seeing the empty doll's bed.

Rescorla found that the majority of children's overextensions were categorical and relatively few were purely analogical. Try your hand at this kind of analysis by typing each of the following cases in this way. For **categorical** extensions, state the name of the category. For **analogical** extensions, state the functional or physical feature on which the analogy is based. For **statements** try to say what sort of statement the child is making.

a. Uses *fly* to refer to flies, specks of dirt, bread-crumbs and his own toes.

b. Says *Mummy* on seeing her mother's coat hanging in the closet.

c. Says *doggie* on seeing lambs, horses, cats and cows.

d. Uses *bubby* (brother) to refer to his brother, 3-year-old boy cousin, and baby boy next door.

e. Says *ball* on seeing both radishes and a stone sphere in a park.

f. Says *car* on seeing trucks, motorcycles and airplanes. Later, she refers to planes as *sky cars*.

g. Says *apple* while looking at the refrigerator.

h. refers to a floating leaf as a *boat*.

i. Says *chocolate* when eating sugar, grapes, figs and cakes.

2.6 Using **Corpus II:5**, find two instances where the child uses an expression unlikely to be used by an adult in that context.

2.7 a. Identify the clear overextension in **Corpus III**.

b. What type of overextension is it? (See **Exercise 2.5**.)

2.8 a. Using **Corpus IV**, find two instances where objects or persons are seemingly 'mislabelled'.

b. For the earlier instance, what qualities does the person named share with the actual object?

c. For the later error, what qualities does the person named by the child share with the person required in this context?

SUPPLE-MENTARY EXERCISES

2.9 Discuss possible explanations for the overextensions you found in **Exercises 2.6**, **2.7** and **2.8**.

2.10 Up until now the overextensions that we have been looking at have been based fairly consistently on similarities between the new objects and the original use of the word. But sometimes children form a chain of associations that start from the original but can then become based on new additions to the chain rather than the original object. For the two cases below, try to follow the children's thinking by connecting up their various uses of *duck* and *cookie*. (The uses are given in the order of their appearance.) Then consider this question: How might such loose and shifting relationships between words and the objects they represent reflect an early misconception that children have about the way language works?

    a. *duck*: a duck swimming in a pond; a cup of milk; a coin with an eagle on it; teddy bear's eye.

    b. *cookie*: cookies; phonograph records; all music.

2.11 In **Corpus III:1–3**, the child is uttering one word at a time, but she clearly has bigger statements in mind. For each dialogue, use the surrounding context to expand the words into full statements.

2.12 Why might parents be more likely to notice cases of over-extension rather than cases of underextension?

2.13 How would you characterize the labelling error in **Corpus VI:6**? Would you class the child's mis-labellings in **Corpus VI:10** as over-extensions?

3

BUILDING UP A DICTIONARY

In Unit 2 we looked primarily at children learning the meaning of nouns like *cat* and *ball*. Here we look at how they tackle verbs and adjectives and how they start building up important meaning links between words.

EXERCISE ✎

3.1 How would you characterize the errors made by these 3–4-year-olds?

> Child A: (building a house with bricks) I'm going to put the house here. I'm not going to put it too tall.
>
> Child B: Sissy took my scissors. (tearing up some paper) I need to take this smaller.
>
> Child C: Mark put my doll in the toilet! (asking for her doll) Put me my dolly. Give me the forks. (setting the table) I'll give the spoons here.

Comment

First of all, you will have noticed that all the errors have involved the verbs used by the children. Child A uses *put* correctly in the first instance, but he also uses it where we would expect a different verb, *make*. Child B does the same thing with take and make. Child C sometimes confuses the verbs *put* and *give*.

As adults, we tend to take the meanings and appropriate usages of these common words for granted, but if we analyse their meanings in a bit more detail, we can gain a greater understanding of how such errors can occur in young children and of the tasks facing them as they build up a dictionary of their native language.

14

Both *put* and *take* involve someone causing something or someone else to change **location**. For example:

    a. Tina put the chair in the corner.
    b. Bill took Annie to the zoo.

In **a.** Tina has caused the chair to change its location and in **b.** Bill has caused Annie to change her location.

The verb *make* also involves someone or something causing a change in something else, but this time it involves a change of **state** rather than a change of **location**:

    c. The advertisement made Annie angry.
    d. Tina made the room tidy.
    e. Bill made a cake.

In **c.** the advertisement has caused a change in Annie's emotional state. In **d.** Tina has caused a change in the room's physical state. And in **e.** Bill has caused the cake to go from a state of nonexistence to one of existence.

✏ **EXERCISE**

3.2 Try doing this same sort of analysis to reveal the similarities and differences between *put* and *give*.

Comment

Both *put* and *give* involve someone causing something else to undergo a kind of change of location:

    f. Bill put the book on the table.
    g. Bill gave the book to Annie.

In **f.** the book has been transferred to the table, while in **g.** the book has been transferred to Annie. But *give* unlike *put* usually involves transfer to a person rather than to a place. In addition, notice that in the *give* example we can say that now Annie has the book, while it would be distinctly odd in the *put* example to say that now the table has the book. In other words, *give* usually involves not only a transfer of location but also a transfer of possession. (In our discussion we pointed out the meaning **similarity** between *put* and *take*; now I'll leave it to you to think about the **difference** between these two verbs.)

As you can see, although the verbs we have been discussing here differ in crucial but sometimes subtle ways, they also share several components of meaning. The errors that children make in their usage are a reflection of the gradual process of learning the subtle distinctions between them just as they needed to learn the distinction between *car* and *truck* or *cake* and *biscuit*.

EXERCISE ✎

3.3 How would you characterize these errors?

Child A: I'm just going to fall this on her. (holding a toy over her baby sister)
Child B: You come my car over here, please.
Child C: I'm swimming my duck. (pushing a toy duck around in the bath)

Comment

Again, the children in these examples are using verbs in ways that differ from adult usage, and again a closer meaning analysis of the words involved reveals a pattern. Notice that in all three cases, the children are using the verbs in the sense of *make it fall, come, swim*. Bowerman's (1982a) study of her daughters' vocabulary development led her to the observation that these errors most commonly occur once children have developed a fairly large vocabulary and have begun to notice regular patterns in their language. They then begin to test the limits of these regularities. If you think about it, there are many verbs in English which do have the ability to be used both with and without the meaning element *make* or *cause*. Here are three examples. I'm sure you can think of many more:

Happen	*Cause to happen*
The door opened.	I opened the door.
The water boiled.	I boiled the water.
She sat down.	I sat her down.

Now, consider the following dialogue.

Experimenter: What is the opposite of tall?
3-year-old: Little.

Was this 3-year-old entirely wrong? In **Unit 1**, we saw that there is a class of words which can be used to describe a wide range of people and objects. Common adjectives such as *nice*, *dirty* and *big* are often amongst the first fifty or so words in children's vocabularies. The acquisition of the special set of adjectives that refer to spatial extension or size has been extensively studied in pre-school children. Clark (1972) found that some of the SPATIAL ADJECTIVES tend to be more difficult than others for children to acquire. That is, they tend to appear later in children's spontaneous speech and when they first appear they are often confused with other similar adjectives. There seems to be a well-established order of difficulty for these which we reproduce in **Table 3.1.** (Difficulty increases as you move from left to right.)

Spatial adjective

This order reflects both the frequency with which these words are used in speaking to young children and the relative simplicity of the meanings involved. For example, *big/little* is used far more often than *tall/short*, but, as you will see in the next exercise, *tall* is also a slightly more complicated concept than *big*.

Table 3.1 Spatial adjectives: order of acquisition/relative difficulty

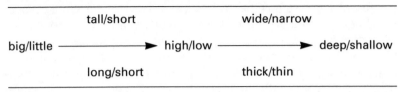

	tall/short		wide/narrow	
big/little	high/low			deep/shallow
	long/short		thick/thin	

✐ **EXERCISE**

3.4 Think in detail about the meaning of *tall*. How is it similar to and different from the meanings of *big*, *long* and *short* ?

Comment

First of all, tall refers to size. As such, it is similar to other words like *big*, *long*, *wide* etc. However, these words differ in terms of the dimensions being described. For example, *big* refers to general size (extension in any direction), but *tall* refers only to vertical extension: *a tall tree*, while *long* refers to horizontal extension: *a long road*. In addition, all these words refer to relative qualities. That is, an object can only be big or tall in relation to something else. A **tall** 3-year-old is still a very **short** human being. This brings us to yet another aspect of the meaning of *tall*. It has an appropriate opposite word, *short*, as do all the spatial adjectives. These pairs express the positive and negative cases of extension. For example:

> *big* = more extension in any direction
> *little* = less extension in any direction
> *small* = less extension in any direction
>
> *tall* = more extension in a vertical direction
> *short* = less extension in a vertical direction

By laying out the meanings like this, we can see that child in our example who used *little* for *short* was not that far off the mark after all. As children grow older, they need to learn even more subtle distinctions between these adjectives and the range of concepts to which they can be applied. For example, *a tall mountain* and *a high mountain* mean virtually the same thing. But do *a tall priest* and *a high priest* mean the same thing? Is *a tall story* the opposite of *a short story*?

We have seen that the tasks facing children as they add new words to their vocabularies go far beyond simply attaching particular strings of sounds to particular concepts. In all languages, words form complex connections with each other which children must gradually discover for themselves. So far in this unit we have seen that words can share several components of their meaning as in *put* and *give* or *big* and *tall*, while others share virtually all their meaning components as in *small* and *little*. Many words have opposite partners which share several of their meaning components but differ as to whether they express positive or negative qualities as in *tall* and *short*. Words often change their meaning to a greater or lesser extent when they are combined with other words in the language as in *a tall man* and *a tall story*. And of course, there are limits to a word's possibilities for combining with other words. Thus, we can use *deep* to describe water, bowls and even people, but we generally do not use this word to describe milk, shoes or tigers.

We turn now to one more important type of meaning connection between words.

EXERCISE ✎

3.5 The following set of terms can all be used to label a particular creature, in this case 'Lassie': *animal, mammal, Lassie, collie, dog, living thing, canine*. Try ordering these terms in a list with the most general term at the top and the most specific term at the bottom.

Comment

Your list should look like this:

> living thing
> animal
> mammal
> canine
> dog
> collie
> Lassie

Many words participate in these kinds of vertical or 'stacking' relationships. Notice that as you move up the list the category membership becomes larger and larger. Notice too, that while we can say that all dogs are mammals, we cannot say that all mammals are dogs.

As children gradually learn about the world around them and gain greater experience with their native language, they eventually build up these sorts of vertical connections. If you have had any experience of talking with young children, you may have noticed that their understanding of the meaning of some higher category terms may differ from that of adults. They may deny that snakes or people are animals or that plants are living things. Similarly, it usually takes some time for children to learn and regularly use the names of some of the more detailed subcategories. For example, 2- to 3-year-olds generally refer to all flowers as *flower*. It is not until they are 4 or 5 that they spontaneously use words like *rose* or *daisy* when shown pictures of the appropriate flower, although at an earlier age, they often understand these words when they hear them spoken.

Children's vocabulary development is one of the most complex and wide-ranging areas of study in language acquisition. However, by the time you finish the exercises at the end of this unit, you will have taken your first steps in this area by applying linguistic analysis to data from children who are engaged in the fascinating enterprise of learning what words mean.

Vocabulary development in 3–4-year-olds involves children making quite subtle meaning distinctions between words such as the difference between *put* and *give* or *big* and *tall*.

Many of the 'errors' at this age suggest that the children have already started to observe and test regular patterns in their language.

In this period children also start to learn about meaning connections between words, such as the connection between *daisy* and *flower* and the differing meanings of *deep* depending on whether it is applied to a puddle or person.

3.6 In **Corpus II:11** Sophie uses an 'unexpected' verb.

a. Which verb is it?
b. Which verb would you probably use in that context?
c. Discuss the similarities in meaning between the child's choice and your choice which might have led to the child's error.

3.7 Find an instance in **Corpus II** where the mother is explicitly trying to help the child build up the kinds of meaning relations discussed in **Exercise 3.5**. Can you think of at least one other appropriate higher category noun that the mother did not include in her description?

3.8 In **Corpus II:20**, Sophie uses two spatial words, *higher* and *upper* as if they were equivalent.

a. Which one of them would you probably use in that context?
b. Think of a sentence context where either of the two words could be used with almost the same meaning.
c. Sophie has also used a third spatial word, *smaller*. To what extent is it an accurate opposite to the other two?

3.9 In **Corpus II:15**, Sophie uses *first* and *best* as if they had identical meanings.

a. Which of the two words you would use in that context?
b. In what ways are the words are similar in meaning and in what ways do they differ?

3.10 Corpus V, Dialogues 3 and **6** and the first sentence of **Dialogue 10** each contain an example of a child using a verb whose **meaning** is inappropriate for that context. For each example state:

a. the verb which has been used inappropriately;
b. the verb an adult would have used in that context;
c. the similarities and differences in meaning between the child's choice and the adult choice.

3.11 Corpus V: 13 and **16** each contain similar errors of word usage. What words have been used inappropriately? How would you characterize these errors?

3.12 Look again at **Exercise 3.3**. In two out of the three examples, you could give the child another verb which does mean *cause that to happen*. For example, if the child had said *She needs to STAY him there*, you could supply *She needs to KEEP him there*. For each of the two cases in **Exercise 3.3**, supply the appropriate verb.

3.13 Now that you have completed **Units 2** and **3**, you should be in a better position to tackle the 'food for thought' in **Unit 1**, p. 4. How would you characterize each of those four 'errors'?

3.14 In **Corpus II:3** Sophie confuses *look* and *find*. In **Corpus II:17** she confuses *hear* and *think*. In **Corpus IV:3** Kathryn confuses *look* and *see*. In **Corpus V:1** Jamie confuses *yesterday* and *tomorrow*. Look up each of these word pairs in a good dictionary and observe the meaning similarities and differences.

3.15 To what extent do you agree with the order of meaning complexity for spatial adjectives given in **Table 3.1**? Do you think that meaning complexity might have an influence on the frequency with which these words are used in speech to young children? Why?

3.16 These children were given the adjectives in the first column (which appear in bold) and were asked to make their puppet say the opposite. Below are the results for three 3-year-olds and three 6-year-olds.

	3-year-olds			*6-year-olds*		
	A. male	B. female	C. male	D. female	E. female	F. male
big	little	small	little	little	little	little
tall	small	short	small	short	short	short

high	down	up	small	low	small	low
long	small	short	big	short	short	short
wide	little	thin	long	thin	skinny	thin
thick	little	thin	small	thin	thin	thin

To what extent do these results agree with the proposed order of difficulty in **Table 3.1**? What similarities and differences do you observe between the 3-year-olds and the 6-year-olds? How do you explain B's response to **high** and C's response to **wide** and **long**?

3.17. In **Corpus VI:3**. Hannah uses an 'unexpected verb'. Analyse this verb using the method in **Exercise 3.6**.

4 PUTTING TOGETHER SENTENCES

We analyse children's first sentences in terms of the types of words
they contain and the meaning relations they express. We also look
at the uses to which children put their first sentences.

EXERCISE ✎

4.1 Compare Timmy's utterances in **Dialogues 1** and **2** and **3** and **4**.
How have they changed?

1. (Age 1;3) Timmy is
pushing his toy car:

Timmy: Car.
Mother: Nice Car!
Timmy: Go.
Mother: Where's it going?

2. (Age 1;11) Timmy is
pushing his toy car:

Timmy: Car go.
Mother: It's going very fast.

3. (Age 1;3) Timmy has just
finished his juice:

Timmy: Juice.
Mother: That's apple juice.
Timmy: More!
Mother: Okay.

4. (Age 1;11) Timmy has just
finished his juice:

Timmy: More juice.
Mother: Are you sure?

Comment

In both **1** and **2**, Timmy is expressing the same idea to his mother: his
car is going. Notice, however, that in **1**, he does this by uttering only
one word at a time, while several months later, in **2**, he is able to
combine both words into one sentence. In the process, he eliminates
some of his mother's guess work. We see the same change taking
place in **Dialogues 3** and **4**.

As you saw in **Unit 2**, children's single word utterances can often involve more than simply labelling. In some contexts they seem to imply a whole statement. Towards the end of the one-word stage, more and more of the child's utterances seem to be of this latter type. In this period, the child will often utter a succession of single words in the conversation all of which would appear in one sentence in older children or adults. Around the age of 2 and usually once they have about 50 words in their spoken vocabulary, children begin to put words together into sentences. For quite a while most of these sentences consist of only two words. So much so, that linguists and psychologists often refer to this as THE TWO-WORD STAGE.

The two-word stage

✐ **EXERCISE**

4.2 Look at this dialogue between parent and child. The parent seems to have no trouble understanding the child although she has left out quite a few things that we would include in our sentences if we were expressing the same ideas. What types of words consistently appear in the child's sentences? What sorts of things does she leave out? How can the parent understand her so easily when the child is omitting so many items?

> C: Find dolly.
> P: Hmmm, you did.
> C: Dolly nice.
> P: She is, isn't she?
> C: Dolly bed.
> P: Wish I were in bed . . .
> C: Drop blanky!
> P: I did. Sorry. I'll pick it up.
> C: Dolly sleep?
> P: Yes, she's sleeping now.

Notice that the words which the child consistently includes are those that are the most necessary ones for conveying her message. These CONTENT WORDS refer to the people, things, actions and qualities involved – mainly the nouns, verbs and adjectives. Of course she sometimes leaves out some of these words too, such as the person who finds the doll and the person who dropped the blanket, but these are fairly obvious given the context of the conversation.

Notice that many of the other items she leaves out are required by the grammar of English but contribute relatively little extra information – endings on the verbs as in *dropped* and *sleeping*, and function words. FUNCTION WORDS include ARTICLES (*a*, *the*); PREPOSITIONS (*in*, *on*, *with*, etc.); the verb *to be* (*I AM happy, you ARE silly*, etc.); AUXILIARY VERBS (*DOES run, CAN run, IS running, HAS run* etc.). Children's early sentences have sometimes been characterized as TELEGRAPHIC. The following exercise will illustrate what I mean.

Comment

Content word

Function word
Article
Preposition
Auxiliary verb
Telegraphic

EXERCISE ✎

4.3 Suppose you had to send the following message to your best friend by telegram and were being charged for every individual letter of every word:

> Paris is horrible. I am leaving on Saturday and I need the credit card. Meet me tomorrow at the usual place.

To spend the least amount of money possible and still get your message across, how would you write the telegram?

Comment

You probably produced something like this:

> Paris horrible. Leave Saturday. Need credit card. Meet tomorrow. Usual place.

In the process, you produced sentence structures very similar to those of the child in **Exercise 4.2**. The term 'telegraphic speech' was originally proposed by Roger Brown (1976) and is still a handy way of describing children's early speech. However, it can be misleading if we take it as a description of what goes on inside children's heads. Omitting the function words in a telegram is done by someone who knows what they are leaving out. It is far from clear that children 'know' the words they are leaving out in their early sentences.

EXERCISE ✎

4.4 Look at this child's sentences and the contexts in which they occurred. What do you notice about the word order used by the child? Could you be sure of your interpretation every time if I hadn't included the context?

- a. Mummy book. Read book. (asking for a story)
- b. Bubble allgone. (bubble has just popped)
- c. Mummy chair. My chair. (saying whose chair is whose)
- d. Teddy floor. He sad. (teddy has fallen on the floor)
- e. Pat it. Face cold. (has just touched sister's face)
- f. More juice. Juice cup. (holding out her cup)
- g. Teddy kiss. (has just made teddy 'kiss' the cat)
- h. Kiss teddy. (now child kisses teddy)
- i. This bus. Sit bus. (pretending large box is a bus)

Comment

In each case, although the child has omitted some words, the words which she did use generally occur in the same order as they would in adult sentences, given the context. This has been widely observed in children acquiring English as their native language. In English, word order is very important. *Bill kicked Fred* and *Fred kicked Bill* mean two different things. The only way we know who kicked whom is by the word order. Notice, for example, that here the child has positioned *teddy* in different positions depending on whether teddy was kissed or did the kissing. However, you probably found that without the surrounding context several of these sentences could have more than one interpretation. For example, *Mummy chair* could also have meant *Mummy is on the chair* or *Mummy did something to the chair*.

Roger Brown (1976) and his colleagues studied two-word sentences from children all over the world. They analysed them by the types of MEANING RELATIONS that the children were expressing and found that at the two-word stage the vast majority of children's utterances expressed the same basic set of meaning relations and that whatever word order the children used, they tended to be fairly consistent although the word order sometimes varied from language to language or from child to child.

Meaning relation

Meaning relation	Example	Context
agent + action	*daddy kick*	(dad kicks ball)
action + affected	*throw stick*	(child throws stick)
agent + affected	*me ball*	(child kicks ball)
action + location	*sit chair*	(child sits on chair)
entity + location	*spoon table*	(spoon is on the table)
possessor + possession	*daddy coat*	(points to dad's coat)
entity + attribute	*kitty big*	(sees tigers in zoo)
nomination	*that cake*	(that is a cake)
recurrence	*more ball*	(finds second ball)
negation	*no ball*	(has lost her ball)

NOMINATION involves labelling persons or objects. RECURRENCE expresses the repetition of events. NEGATION can express denial, rejection or non-existence. However, notice that the first seven of these relations involve the **combination** of two terms. The terms AGENT (the do-er), ACTION, AFFECTED (the done-to), LOCATION, ENTITY (person or thing being described or located), ATTRIBUTE (the description), POSSESSOR, POSSESSION all describe different meaning elements which combine to produce the overall meaning of the sentence. A more technical but useful term for these sorts of meaning elements is SEMANTIC ROLE.

Nomination
Recurrence
Negation
Agent
Action
Affected
Location
Entity
Attribute
Possessor
Possession
Semantic role

✐ **EXERCISE**

4.5 Try your hand at this type of analysis by applying it to each of the two-word sentences produced by the children in **Exercises 4.1** and **4.2**.

4.1: *car go* = agent + action
    more juice = recurrence

Comment

4.2: *find dolly* = action + affected
dolly nice = entity + attribute
dolly bed = entity + location
drop blanky = action + affected
dolly sleep = agent + action

If this was the first time you have tried this sort of analysis, you may have found it a bit tricky, but the exercises at the end of the unit will give you more practice. If you go on to read more advanced books on child language, you may find that some authors use slightly different names for some of the these meaning relations and semantic roles, but the basic principle is the same and they usually give examples to illustrate what they are talking about.

Now, suppose I wanted you to close the window. I could say either *Close the window* or *I'm cold*. We could analyse the first sentence as action + affected and the second one as entity + attribute. But what this sort of analysis does not capture is that in both cases I am making the same request. In other words, these sentences mean the same thing in terms of what I am trying to accomplish with language. Take another example. If I say *I'm very busy right now*, I could be making a simple assertion, supplying you with information about myself, or I could be requesting you to go away and leave me alone. The same string of words has been used to accomplish two different goals. We can apply this sort of analysis to children's language as well. Even with children's very early utterances, we can see that they put them to a variety of uses.

EXERCISE ✎

4.6 Look at this data and classify these utterances as either assertions or requests.

1. (ball rolls towards child; child looks at ball)
   Ball!
2. (ball is on high shelf; child reaches towards ball and whines)
   Ball!
3. (child has just finished the last cookie)
   More cookie.
4. (child is watching butterfly; second butterfly appears)
   More butterfly.
5. (child sees armadillo in zoo)
   What that?

Comment

1, 4 are assertions. **2, 3, 5** are requests. Did you notice the difference between the requests made in **2** and **3** and the request in **5**? We could characterize the first two as asking the listener to perform some sort of **action** – getting the ball, supplying another cookie. In **5**, the child is asking the listener to provide **information**, in this case the name of an animal. Obviously, analysing children's utterances in terms of the uses to which they put their language, often referred to as SPEECH ACTS, requires a great deal of detailed information not only about the context in which the utterances were made but also about the child's body language and tone of voice.

Speech act

If you have had much experience of listening to toddlers, you will probably have observed that children at the one-word stage still rely quite heavily on these sorts of extra-linguistic cues to help them make their intentions clear. As vocabulary increases and children are able to encode more and more information in a single sentence, the use of gestures and whining tends to decrease. Children soon learn that language is a very powerful tool indeed.

UNIT SUMMARY

Around the age of 2, children start to put together sentences.

These early sentences usually consist of only two words and are quite telegraphic, consisting mainly of content words: nouns, verbs, adjectives.

Early sentences can be analysed by the meaning relations they express and by the uses to which the children put them.

FURTHER EXERCISES

4.7 Using **Corpus I**, analyse **1**, **3**, **6**, **13**, **16**, **21** in terms of the word classes (noun, verb, adjective) being used and the meaning relations being expressed. Example:

	kiss	*teddy*
word class	verb +	noun
meaning relation	action +	affected

4.8 Using only the two-word utterances in **Corpus I**, find:

   a. Two cases of negation and one of recurrence.
   b. Three cases which (depending on the context) could be analysed as **either** possessor + possession **or** agent + affected.
   c. One case which could be analysed as **either** action + location **or** entity + location.

4.9 Using **Corpus I**, I have expanded the utterances in **1** and **5** into two possible adult versions, depending on the context:

   1a. *Daddy* is *taking* the *banana*.
   1b. Can *Baby take* a *banana*?
   5a. See *Baby's crib*.
   5b. Does *Baby sleep* in the *crib*?

      a. State the semantic role played by each italicized word.

      b. Compare each sentence to the child's version and state which words or parts of words have been added.

      c. For each of the **whole words** that I have added state whether it is a function word or a content word.

SUPPLE-MENTARY EXERCISES ✎

4.10 Analyse each sentence in **Exercise 4.4** in terms of the meaning relations being expressed between the two words.

4.11 Analyse the children's utterances in **Dialogues 2** and **4** in **Exercise 4.1** and in the dialogue in **Exercise 4.2** in terms of the speech acts (assertion, request for action, request for information) involved.

4.12 Look back to Christian's remark at age 2 in **Unit 1** p. 1. What meaning relation was he expressing? What speech act was he performing?

4.13 Pick any three sentences in **Corpus I** and describe the contexts in which the child's utterance could be analysed as an **assertion** and the contexts in which it could be analysed as a **request**.

4.14 In **Corpus VI:1, 2, 8**, Hannah appears to substitute *Uh* for some words. Are these content words or function words?

Copula

4.15 When the verb *to be* is the main verb in a sentence, as in *I AM happy* or *You WERE naughty*, it is called the COPULA. Find the instances in **Corpus VI** where Hannah omits the copula from her sentences.

4.16 Find the instances in **Corpus VI** where Hannah omits **articles**.

4.17 In **Corpus VI:3**, analyse the meaning relations expressed by Hannah in each of her utterances.

BUILDING LONGER SENTENCES

5

In this unit we analyse children's sentences as they become increasingly more complex in structure. We introduce the notion of grammatical role to aid our analysis.

In this unit and the next you will find that children's utterances are sometimes said to be typical of certain 'stages' rather than certain 'ages'. The reason for this is that normal children can differ by many months in the age at which they consistently produce certain types of sentence structures. Roger Brown and his colleagues found that for predicting the kinds of structures that children would use, their average utterance length worked much better than their age. Table 5.1 gives a summary of the normal age ranges for different average utterance lengths.

Table 5.1 Normal age ranges for different average utterance lengths

Age	Length
1;6–2;3	1–2 words
1;9–2;6	2 words
1;11–3;1	2–3 words
2;2–4;0	3–4 words
2;3–4;0	4 words

Towards the end of the two-word stage, children start producing more and more sentences containing three or four words. From here on language really takes off. There is no three-word stage as such. What follows is a period of two to three years of astonishing progress on a variety of fronts. To remind yourself just how astonishing this progress is, compare **Dialogues 3** and **26** in **Corpus II**.

EXERCISE

5.1 Using **Dialogues 1–10** in **Corpus II**, compare the sentences that Sophie is producing with those we were looking at in **Unit 4**. Obviously, they are longer. But look at their structure. In what ways are they similar. How do they differ?

Comment

First of all, we notice that these early three- to four-word sentences are still quite 'telegraphic' in character. Many of the little function words are still omitted. The verbs usually lack any past or present endings. We do notice some significant changes however. First of all, Sophie has started using some prepositions (most noticeably *on*). Articles have begun to appear, although not consistently (see **Dialogue 10**, for example). Second, we notice that Sophie's sentences seem more complete in terms of the way she encodes the meaning relations involved.

EXERCISE

5.2 Using Sophie's first and third sentences in **Corpus II:2**, analyse the meaning relations as you did in **Unit 4**.

Comment

you		take		a bissy	
agent	+	action	+	affected	
you		put		bissy	on there
agent	+	action	+	affected	+ location

In each of these sentences, Sophie has explicitly included **all** the semantic roles involved. Notice that her mother would have understood her just as well if she left one or even two of them out.

It has been observed that as children move beyond the two-word stage, they expand their sentences in at least two ways. Often children will utter three sentences in a row. Each one expressing the same idea. The first two sentences each encode two of the three semantic roles involved, and the third one puts them all together in the same sentence:

Daddy kick.   Kick   ball.   Daddy   kick   ball.
agent + action   action + affected   agent + action + affected

Sit   chair.   Mummy sit.   Mummy sit   chair.
action + location   agent +   action   agent + action + location

Planning and executing a sentence that encodes an event with several participants is quite complicated for the novice language user. You have probably noticed this if you are learning to speak a foreign language. You have to choose and remember the appropriate words, think of the order in which they should come, and put your tongue, lips, vocal cords and lungs into action to produce the whole thing with a 'native accent'. In the early stages it is not surprising that children often have a couple of trial runs before they produce their final version of the sentence.

✎ **EXERCISE**

5.3 How would you characterize what is happening here?

1a. **Get ball.**   1b. **My ball.**   1c. **Get my ball.**
2a. **See kitty.**   2b. **Big kitty.**   2c. **See big kitty.**

Comment

Another way that children start to expand their two-word sentences is by expanding one of the elements that is already there. Using a semantic role analysis we notice that **1a.** consists of action + affected. In **1b.**, the affected has been expanded into possessor + possession. In **1c.** the entire lot has been encoded in one sentence. In **2a.** we have action + affected. In **2b.** the affected has been expanded into attribute + entity. And again, **2c.** puts them all together.

Up to now we have analysed these sentences primarily in terms of meaning relations. But we could also describe what is going on purely in terms of grammatical roles and structures. For example, we can describe *my ball* as a NOUN PHRASE. The most crucial or HEAD WORD in that phrase is the noun *ball*. *My ball* is an expansion of this word. Notice that we can expand such phrases indefinitely: *my ball*, *my red ball*, *my new red ball*, *my big new red ball*. . . . But in all these cases, the whole phrase acts as a single grammatical unit which can fill certain 'slots' or GRAMMATICAL ROLES in a sentence:

Noun phrase
Head word

Grammatical role

> They kicked MY BALL.
> MY BALL was kicked.
> This is MY BALL.
> I sat on MY BALL.

At this stage you may be wondering why we have to make a distinction between grammatical roles and semantic roles. The point is, describing sentences purely in terms of their meaning relations does not capture all the facts about the way English works, or for that matter, about the way any language works. Children would not get very far if they continued to construct their sentences purely in terms of meaning relations, although there is some evidence that, initally, children learning English may be using rules like 'agent comes first' or 'action comes before affected'. The following two exercises should help make my point.

EXERCISE ✎

5.4 Look at sentences **a.–e.**, and assign semantic roles to each of the underlined segments. Then ask yourself the following questions: Does the agent always precede the action? Is it the agent that determines whether the verb will be in a singular or plural form (*is* vs *are*, for example)? Would you have been entirely happy analysing *like* and *want* as actions? Would you have been entirely happy analysing *Bill* and *Tina* as agents?

    a. <u>The big boys</u> <u>are kicking</u> <u>my ball</u>.
    b. <u>My ball</u> <u>is being kicked</u> <u>by the big boys</u>.
    c. Bill liked my ball.
    d. Tina wanted my ball.
    e. Annie kicked my ball.

Comment

You will have noticed that in both **a.** and **b.**, *the big boys* were the agents and that *my ball* was the affected. In the process, you will probably have observed that the agent does not always come before the action and that the agent does not always determine the form of the verb which is expressing that action. If it did, **b.** would be *My ball are being kicked by the big boys*. What unites the phrase *the big boys* in **a.** and the phrase *my ball* in **b.** is that each one determines the form of the verb within its sentence. In other words, they may not be filling the same semantic role but they are filling the same grammatical

Subject

role which we call SUBJECT. Now in **c.** and **d.**, have *Bill* or *Tina* actually done anything to *my ball*? Have they changed, moved, or affected it in any way simply by liking or wanting it? *Want* and *like* do not really seem to be actions in the sense that *kick* is an action. And yet *kick*, *want* and *like* all fit into the same position in the word order. All three of them are the words in the sentence that can be marked with the *-ed* ending to indicate past time. Although we cannot really capture their similarity by saying that they are all actions, we can capture it by simply saying that all three of them are **verbs**.

At this point we need to make one more 'technical distinction'. We need to make a distinction between the semantic role, **affected** (a person or thing which has moved, changed or been affected in some

Direct object

way through an action), and the grammatical role, DIRECT OBJECT of the verb, which is something rather different as you will soon see.

EXERCISE ✎

5.5 In each of the following two sentences pick which form of the pronoun you would use and then state which of the words in that sentence is the **affected**.

    a. He/Him was kicked by the girls.
    b. The girls kicked he/him.

Then look at the following three sentences and pick which form of the pronoun you would use. Are there any true **affecteds** in these sentences? How did you know which pronoun to use?

    c. I want he/him.
    d. She likes he/him.
    e. They know he/him.

Your choices probably were: **a.** *He*; **b.** *him*; **c.** *him*; **d.** *him*; **e.** *him*.   **Comment**
But in **a.** *He* is the affected, while in **b.** *him* is the affected. In **c.**, **d.**, and **e.** there were no true affecteds at all. It seems that the notion of affected is not really very helpful in terms of deciding which pronoun form to use. Yet you were able to choose the correct ones quite easily. We can capture the similarity between sentences **b.**, **c.**, **d.** and **e.** by saying that in each case *him* is the **direct object** of the verb. Notice too, that **c.**, **d.** and **e.**, each contain two pronouns. Had I asked you, you would have easily chosen the correct form for the other pronoun in the sentence. What unites *He* in **a.**, *I* in **c.**, *She* in **d.** and *They* in **e.** is that they are all grammatical subjects, irrespective of whether or not they are agents.

In the last two exercises we have seen that semantic roles and grammatical roles are not necessarily the same. We have also seen that by analysing sentences in terms of grammatical roles we can make much more reliable predictions about the way English works, such as:

1 In standard English sentences, the verb precedes its direct object.
2 The verb will agree in person and number with the noun phrase that constitutes the grammatical subject.
3 We use the pronoun forms *I, you, he, she, it, we* and *they* when these words are in the subject position, and we use the forms *me, you, him, her, it, us* and *them* when these words are in the direct object position.

As adult speakers of English, we 'know' rules like these and many more besides. This rule system allows us to produce and understand the infinite number of possible sentences in our language reliably, effortlessly and at great speed. This is the rule system that children ultimately acquire. Of course, most people are not particularly aware of the types of rules that we have been talking about in this unit. Once learned, they become as automatic as walking. If they were not so automatic, the simplest conversation would take forever! If you have survived the last two exercises intact, you will be more consciously aware of these rules. You can talk and write about them, and you can use them to analyse data from children who are still in the process of acquiring the sentence structure of their native language.

Exactly how children manage to build up such an abstract rule system for themselves is still an open question. We do know that along the way they construct temporary systems for themselves. The following exercise will give you a flavour of how linguistic analysis can reveal this process.

EXERCISE ✎

5.6 Here are some data from a study of one child learning how to use the pronoun that refers to himself. Ursula Bellugi (1971) found that Adam seemed to go through three stages in the process. Look at the data and then try to characterize the rule that he is using at each stage. You can assume that these are representative samples from each stage.

> Stage I
> Adam home. Adam go hill.
> Like Adam book shelf. Pick Adam up.

> Stage II
> I like drink it. I Adam driving. I making coffee.
> Wake me up. Why hitting me?
> What me doing? Why me spilled it?

> Stage III
> That what I do. Can I put them on.
> You want me? You watch me.

Comment

In **Stage I**, Adam, like many young children, refers to himself by his own name regardless of where it occurs in the sentence. **Stage II** presents a more interesting problem. Here Adam seems to have learned that *I/me* is the way people generally refer to themselves when they speak. He has also learned that this pronoun seems to change its form depending on where it occurs in the sentence. We notice that Adam uses *I* when it is the first word in the sentence and uses *me* when it comes at any other point. Now, if you looked at all the sentences you produced in a day which contained *I/me* you would observe that that most of the time *I* appears as the first word and that *me* predominates in successive positions. Adam's rule seems to work most of the time. He produces many adult-like sentences in terms of pronoun use. But he also produces errors like *What me doing?* and *Why me spilled it?* It is not a reliable rule. The rule, as we saw in **Exercise 5.5**, is that *I* occurs in **subject** position, which is usually, but not always, the first word in the sentence, as we can see here:

> a. Tomorrow I am leaving.
> b. What on earth am I doing?

We know that *I* is the subject in both **a.** and **b.** because the verb *to be* takes its form *am* to agree with the subject. In **Stage III** Adam has acquired this grown-up rule of English. He no longer bases his choice on simple word order, but on something more abstract – whether or not the pronoun is filling the subject role in the sentence.

What we have seen is a child going far beyond simple imitation. If he were simply imitating his parents and other adults, he would never have produced *What me doing?* Adults do not produce sentences like that. Adam has actively constructed rules for himself, based on his observations and revised in light of his growing experience.

UNIT SUMMARY

The average length of a child's utterances is a much better predictor than age of the types of sentence structures that the child will be using.

After the two-word stage children's sentences become increasingly longer. They also become more complex in terms of the number of meaning relations they express and the grammatical structures they use.

In sentences, the semantic role and the grammatical role played by a phrase are not necessarily the same. In this period children start to use rule systems which are grammatically rather than semantically based.

The grammatical errors that children make can reveal the kinds of rule systems that they are actively constructing for themselves.

FURTHER EXERCISES

5.7 In **Corpus II:6**, Sophie provides an example of one of the kinds of expansion processes that frequently occur in children's early attempts at producing longer sentences.

> a. Analyse her first three sentences in that dialogue in terms of the semantic roles which they encode.
> b. To what extent is her word choice for **agent** an error?

5.8 Using **Corpus II:1–10,**

> a. Find an instance where Sophie utters a one-word sentence and immediately follows it by a three-word expanded version.
> b. Analyse both sentences in terms of the meaning relations expressed.
> c. What **preposition** is Sophie omitting?

5.9 Using **Corpus II:1–10,**

> a. Find an example of Sophie using a **noun phrase** on its own in one sentence and then immediately incorporating it into the following sentence.
> b. The second sentence still lacks a **preposition** – which one?

5.10 In **Corpus II:8**, Sophie is trying to construct a very complicated sentence.

> a. Write a single sentence that expresses the idea she is trying to convey.
> b. What makes this sentence so complicated? How does Sophie solve her problem?

5.11 Using **Corpus II**:

> a. Discuss two different types of errors that Sophie makes with the pronoun *she/her*.
> b. Does this give us any clue to the source of her error in **Exercise 5.7**? Some background information: Sophie has two sisters and no brothers.

5.12 Many toddlers perform little monologues just before they fall asleep. It is a kind of verbal play, but it can also reflect the areas of language that the child is working on. The data below are from Ruth Weir (1962), who placed a tape-recorder in her children's bedroom each evening before they fell asleep. In each case state which area or areas the child seems to be 'rehearsing'.

a.		b.	
	Go for glasses.		Take the monkey.
	Go for them.		Take it.
	Go to the top.		Stop it.
	Go for blouse.		Stop the ball.
	Go for shoes.		Stop it.

5.13 Look at Hannah's last utterance in **Corpus VI:10** and expand that utterance to an adult version giving the meaning she was trying to convey. (See **Exercise 4.9** for guidance.) Compare your version and Hannah's. Which semantic and grammatical roles has Hannah omitted? Which ones has she included?

SAYING 'NO' AND ASKING QUESTIONS

6

We describe the rules for forming negative sentences and asking both Yes/No and WH questions in English. We then analyse data from children at various stages in the acquisition of these rules.

In **Unit 4** we observed that in communication terms, function words carry far less information than the content words. The way we pronounce these words when speaking a sentence reflects this.

✐ **EXERCISE**

6.1 Say each of the following sentences out loud as if you were in a conversation with someone. Were some words pronounced more distinctly than others? Which ones?

    a. The cat is jumping.
    b. Annie will leave from the station.
    c. Bill has painted the house white.

Comment

You probably noticed that *cat, jumping, Annie, leave, station, Bill, painted, house* and *white* (the content words) were spoken a bit more loudly and distinctly than *the, a, is, will, from* and *has* (the function words). For some of these words, the **auxiliary verbs**, it probably seemed more natural to say *The cat's jumping, Annie'll leave, Bill's painted*, reducing the number of sounds the auxiliaries contain and attaching them to the preceding word. This process is called CONTRACTION. Although the main verb in a sentence carries the basic information as to the action or state under discussion, auxiliary verbs modify the meaning of the main verb in a variety of ways. Compare *I play chess* to: *I AM playing chess, I MIGHT play chess, I WILL play*

Contraction

chess, I SHOULD play chess, I HAVE played chess, I CAN play chess. In English, these auxiliary verbs are crucial for producing the standard forms for saying *no* and asking questions.

EXERCISE ✎

Negative

6.2 Turn each of these sentences into its NEGATIVE counterpart. Try to characterize the overall procedure you followed.

Example: I should stay./I should not stay.

a. You can leave.   e. He wanted them.
b. They will leave.   f. He wants them.
c. She is leaving.   g. We are nice.
d. He has left.

Comment

First of all you added *not*. In **a.–d.**, you placed *not* just after the auxiliary verb. In spoken language, we would normally contract it on to the auxiliary: *can't, won't, isn't, hasn't*. In **e.** and **f.** you had to add a special auxiliary *do*. Notice that when you did this, the marking for TENSE (past or present time) moved from the main verb to the auxiliary: *doesn't want, didn't want*. In **g.** *are* is the main verb, but in most dialects of English the verb *to be* does not require an extra auxiliary: *We aren't nice* not *We don't be nice*.

Tense

Now that we have spelled out the procedure for forming negatives, we can start analysing data from an American child at three stages in his progress towards the adult form of negative sentences. His stages are fairly typical of English-speaking children.

EXERCISE ✎

6.3 Try to characterize the rule which the child uses in each of the first two stages. The typical length of the child's sentences at each stage is given in square brackets.

Stage I [2–3 words]

a. No wipe finger.   d. Wear mitten no.
b. No singing song.   e. No the sun shining.
c. More no.   f. Not a teddy bear.

Stage II [3–4 words]

a. I can't catch you.   d. I don't want it.
b. I no want envelope.   e. Don't leave me.
c. He not little. He big.   f. No pinch me!

One way of analysing this data was proposed by Ursula Bellugi (1967). In **Stage I** the child is employing a fairly simple rule. Use *no* or *not* (usually *no*) and attach it to either the beginning or the end of the sentence. At this stage his affirmative sentences are also very short and telegraphic – auxiliary verbs are absent as is the main verb *to be*. In **Stage II**, we notice that most of the time *no/not* goes **inside** the sentence. We notice the continuing absence of the main verb *to be* as in **c.**, but we also see that sentences **a.**, **d.** and **e.** are quite adult-like. We have *not* seemingly attached to the auxiliary and *do* added where required in sentences **d.** and **e.** But compare these to sentences **b.** and **f.** which encode similar ideas but simply insert *no* inside the sentence. Before, I said 'seemingly attached' because auxiliaries like *can*, *will* and *do* never appear on their own in the child's affirmative sentences at this stage. At first children think of *can't*, *don't*, *won't* simply as alternative forms of *not* rather than as a combination of *can/do/will* + *not*. So, at this stage we find sentences like **b.** and **d.** and **e.** and **f.** co-existing.

By **Stage III** (typical sentence length over four words), auxiliary verbs appear in affirmative sentences as well as negative ones, the verb *to be* appears where required much more frequently and the sentences have generally become more complex and complete. Here are some sample negatives from **Stage III**.

Comment

> Stage III
>
> I gave him some so he won't cry.
> I am not a doctor.
> No, I don't have a book.

He is getting very close to an adult-like rule system for forming negative sentences. But there are still a few wrinkles to be ironed out.

✐ **EXERCISE**

6.4 Here are some errors from **Stage III**. What problems does the child still need to solve?

a. You didn't caught me.   d. I isn't . . . I not sad.
b. I not hurt him.   e. I don't never do that.
c. That not turning.

Children can take quite a while to get the hang of the *do* auxiliary – knowing when to add it and moving the tense marking from the main verb to *do*. In **a.** the child marks past tense on both the main verb and the auxiliary, while in **b.** the *do* was omitted. The verb *to be* has been omitted in **c.** and **d.** Both *to be* used as main verb (*I AM not sad*) and as auxiliary verb (*I AM not turning*) take some time to appear consistently even in affirmative sentences, partly because this verb has so many different other forms to be memorized: *am*, *are*, *is*, *was*, *were*,

Comment

been, being. With the added complexity of negative sentences, *be* can sometimes be omitted well into the third stage. Sentence **e.** contains a double negative. English has other words which can make a sentence negative besides *not*, for example: *I NEVER see him*; *I saw NOBODY.* One of the rules of Standard American and British English is that negation can appear only once in a sentence. Thus *I didn't see nobody* and *I don't never see him* are considered ungrammatical. Of course, this rule is not a universal one. In many of the world's languages and in some dialects of English the double negative is not only permitted, it is obligatory! Since this child is acquiring Standard American English, he still needs to sort out the appropriate use of these other negative words.

Even at the one-word stage, children ask questions, signalling their intent with the same tone of voice adults use for questions as in *More?, Kitty?, Daddy?, No?, Chair?, Juice?* But learning to ask questions the way adults do can be quite a complicated business for the child acquiring English. And again, auxiliary verbs are very important. We start first with YES/NO QUESTIONS.

Yes/No question

EXERCISE ✎

6.5 Turn each of these sentences into a Yes/No question: *I should go/Should I go?* Then try to characterize the procedure you followed.

    a. You saw him.
    b. I can run.
    c. She is nice.
    d. He will leave.
    e. He is running.

Comment

Having produced *Did you see him?*, *Can I run?*, *Is she nice?*, *Will he leave?*, and *Is he running?*, you will have noticed that in Yes/No questions the order of the grammatical subject and the auxiliary verb is reversed. Where the equivalent statement has no auxiliary as in **a.**, *do* is added with the tense marking moving from main verb to auxiliary, as it does in negative sentences. As with negative sentences, the verb *to be* does not require an extra auxiliary. Until auxiliary verbs and the verb *to be* start to appear consistently in children's ordinary statements, they continue to produce Yes/No questions like *See my doggie?*, *You can't fix it?*, *You sad?*

Once children start using auxiliaries in their statements, then Yes/No questions start taking the adult form, although as with negative sentences, they still produce errors at this stage like *Oh, did I caught it?*

✐ **EXERCISE**

6.6 Here we look at another type of question. Make up full sentence *answers* for each of these questions and then try to characterize the procedure for forming WH QUESTIONS like these.

WH question

    a. What will you see?
    b. Where did you see *Hamlet*?
    c. Why are you seeing *Hamlet*?
    d. When can you see *Hamlet*?
    e. Who saw *Hamlet*?

Yours were undoubtedly similar . . .

Comment

    a. I will see **Hamlet**.
    b. I saw *Hamlet* **at the Old Vic Theatre**.
    c. I am seeing *Hamlet* **because it's a new production**.
    d. I can see *Hamlet* **tomorrow**.
    e. **I** saw *Hamlet*.

WH questions cannot be appropriately answered by saying *yes* or *no*. They ask for specific bits of information which I have bolded in my answers. Notice that the relevant pieces of information fill different functions in the reply sentences: **a.** direct object; **b.** location; **c.** reason; **d.** time; **e.** subject. To form these questions the appropriate WH word which signals the type of information required is placed at the front of the sentence, followed by the auxiliary verb (adding *do* if no other auxiliary is used), followed by the subject. There is one exception. When the grammatical subject is being questioned as in **e.**, the subject and auxiliary are not reversed.

✐ **EXERCISE**

6.7 Here are some typical WH questions that children produce at three stages with some of their Yes/No questions from the same stage. What differences do you notice in the way the children structure these two types of sentences?

Yes/No	*WH*
Stage I [2–3 words]	
See hole? Sit chair?	What that? Where Mama?
Jamie water?	What doing? Who that?
Stage II [3–4 words]	
See my doggie?	What me think?
That black too?	Why you smiling?
I have it?	Where me sleep?
You can't fix it?	Why not me drink it?

Yes/No   *WH*

Stage III [over 4 words]
Does lions walk?   Where my spoon goed?
Will you help me?   Why the tree going?
Can't you work this thing?   Why kitty can't stand up?
Oh, did I caught it?   What I did yesterday?

Comment

Children start using *what* and *where* quite early on. From the very beginning they usually put the WH word at the front of the sentence. *What that?* and *What doing?* are common questions at this age. Children seem to use them as a vocabulary learning tool, in the sense of *Tell me the name for that thing or action.* In **Stage II**, *why* makes its appearance and longer sentences are produced. Auxiliary verbs are usually absent although their negative counterparts (*can't/don't*) start to appear in Yes/No questions. In **Stage III**, we see a marked difference between the two types of questions. While most of the time the subject and auxiliary are reversed in Yes/No questions, WH questions do not yet show this reversal.

EXERCISE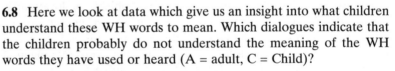

6.8 Here we look at data which give us an insight into what children understand these WH words to mean. Which dialogues indicate that the children probably do not understand the meaning of the WH words they have used or heard (A = adult, C = Child)?

  a. A: Look at that car.
     C: Why that a car?
     A: Because it is, that's why. There's another one.
     C: Why there's nother one?
     A: Oh, Jamie!

  b. A: You can't have that.
     C: Why I can't have that?

  c. A: Where's the deer going?
     C: Because he is.

  d. C: Lost my truck. Where my truck go?
     A: Here it is.

  e. A: Who did you hit?
     C: Hit.

  f. A: What are you writing?
     C: Arm.

  g. A: Who do you love?
     C: Mommy. You. I love fishy too.

  h. A: What do you need?
     C: Need some chocolate.

The dialogues with inappropriate use or understanding of WH words were: **a.**, **c.**, **e.** and **f.** *Why* asks for the cause or reason involved in a proposition. Notice the inappropriate use of *why* in **a.** which is very typical of young children, as is the response of the exasperated parent. Compare this to **b.**, where *why* is used appropriately. *Where* questions the location of the action. Compare **c.** where the child gives an inappropriate answer (a reason) to **d.** in which *where* is used appropriately. Now compare the children's responses in **e.** and **f.** to those in **g.** and **h.** In **e.** and **f.** *who* and *what* were questioning the objects of the verbs: the person being hit, the thing being written. But in **e.** the child repeats the verb, and in **f.** answers with something used to carry out the action or possibly its location, if he is writing on his arm. In **g.** and **h.** the children have responded appropriately with the objects of the verb: *love **Mommy**, need **some chocolate**.*

It appears that in the early stages children understand that WH words signal questions, and that they need to respond with information rather than a simple yes or no. But it takes some time to sort out the meaning of the various WH words and the appropriate ways to use and respond to them. By now, you are thoroughly familiar with the Corpus and you will have observed that children ask many questions. This is partly because they need to find out about the world, partly because they want to keep the conversation going and partly because they are simply practising the art of asking questions.

UNIT SUMMARY

In English the acquisition of auxiliary verbs is crucial for producing the adult forms of both negative sentences and questions.

Children appear to go through several stages in learning how to form questions and negatives.

The adult form of Yes/No questions tends to be acquired earlier than for WH questions, and some types of WH questions appear to be easier than others. *Where* questions tend to be the first ones to be produced and understood by children.

🖉 **FURTHER EXERCISES**

6.9 For each negative sentence in **Corpus I**, state the rule used for the placement of *no/not*. Indicate those which conform to the **Stage II** description in **Exercise 6.3**.

6.10 When studying children's early negative sentences, Lois Bloom (1970) classified them according to three different meanings of *no/not*: REJECTION or refusal of a request or an action; the NON-EXISTENCE or absence of something; DENIAL of the truth or accuracy of a statement. Use this analysis to classify the negatives in the following Corpus

Rejection
Non-existence
Denial

dialogues (context given where necessary): **I:2** (has just been told to sit down); **I:8** (responding to *there's a blue one*); **I:12** (has been put in bed for a nap); **I:18** (holding a broken cup); **II:3**, **18**, **19**; **III:2**, **4** and **5**; **V:13**.

6.11 List the all the auxiliary verbs used by: Sophie in **Corpus II:20**, Alison in **Corpus III:6** and Kathryn in **Corpus IV:3**.

6.12 State the nature of the errors in question and negative formation in **Corpus V:2**, **9** and **14**. Assume the children are acquiring Standard American or British English.

6.13 Find a dialogue in **Corpus II** where Sophie produces two consecutive WH questions using *what* to question the object of the verb. State the verbs in each case.

SUPPLE-MENTARY EXERCISES ✎

6.14 What evidence do you have in **Corpus II:19** that Sophie is using an adult-like rule for forming negatives?

6.15 a. In **Corpus II:1–10**, does Sophie appear to understand *who* and *what* when they question the subject? Cite supporting examples.
   b. In **Corpus II:1–10** can we be sure she fully understands *when* and *why*? Cite examples.
   c. Cite examples in **Corpus II:11–26** where *why* is used appropriately.
   d. *When* can also be used in constructions like: *I knew him **when he was young***. Cite three examples in **Corpus II:11–26** where Sophie uses *when* in this way and one example of her using it appropriately to ask a time question.
   e. In the Corpus, at what age does Sophie first produce an appropriate *where* question?

6.16 Because the construction of WH questions is quite complex, children often make several false starts and hesitations and produce errors that do not occur in their simpler sentences. This is especially true if they have other complicated words or structures to deal with at the same time. **Dialogues II:13** and **14** provide an illustration of this. Make a detailed analysis of these dialogues in terms of the errors made and the nature of the 'extra complications' involved. You may want to look again at **Units 2–5** to get ideas and techniques for your analysis.

6.17 In **Exercise 6.7**, we noted that subject/auxiliary reversal tends to occur later in children's WH questions than in their Yes/No questions. Why might this be the case?

6.18 Using **Corpus VI:1–9**, at what stage for forming negatives would you put Hannah and why?

6.19 Using all of **Corpus VI**, is there any evidence that Hannah understands and uses *what*, *where* and *why* questions appropriately?

7 BECOMING A WORD MAKER

We analyse data from children who are mastering some of the processes for altering the form of words in different sentence contexts and for coining new words to fill gaps in their vocabulary: suffixing, prefixing, compounding and conversion.

In our discussion of 'telegraphic speech', we mentioned that in children's early sentences the nouns and verbs often appear without the endings that adult speakers would use in those contexts:

> drop blanket (You dropp*ed* the blanket.)
> kitty big (Those kittie*s* are big.)
> Mummy chair (This is Mummy*'s* chair.)

Looking through the Corpus, you will have noticed that as children get older, as their vocabulary increases, and as their sentences become more complex, these endings start to appear. You will also have noticed the children producing words like *putted*. *Putted* is an error, but a very clever one as we shall see.

EXERCISE

7.1 Here are some verbs that I guarantee you have never seen before because I have made them up. Fill in the blanks by saying the appropriate word *out loud*.

> a. I like to tark, so yesterday I <u>tarked</u>.
> b. I like to droom, so yesterday I _____ .
> c. I like to lunt, so yesterday I _____ .
> d. I like to zond, so yesterday I _____ .

Now, fill in the blanks for these real verbs.

> e. I wanted to go, so yesterday I _____ .

f. I wanted to speak, so yesterday I _____ .
g. I wanted to hit him, so yesterday I _____ him.

Comment

For **a.–d.** to indicate PAST TENSE you added something that would be written as *-ed*. But did you notice that all these *-ed*s did not sound the same? With *tark* you added a **t** sound (*tarkt*), with *droom* you added a **d** sound (*droomd*) and with *lunt* and *zond*, words that already end with a **t** or **d** sound, you added something like **id** (*luntid* and *zondid*). The pronunciation of this ending varies according the last sound of the words to which it attached. How were you able to do this with verbs you have never seen before? Somewhere along the line (before you were 5 years old, in fact) you learned an important rule of English WORD FORMATION. So, if that is the rule, why did you use *went* instead of *goed*, *spoke* instead of *speaked*, and *hit* instead of *hitted*? Somewhere along the line you also learned that the general rule has some exceptions.

    When children learn a word-formation rule like this, they need to have observed that the **t/d/id** sounds on the ends of words are not just extra sounds – they consistently add an extra bit of meaning. In this case they add the meaning *past*. And they are detachable sounds. They can be used with virtually all verbs to alter their meaning in the same way. Linguists refer to these sorts of endings as SUFFIXES.

    Unfortunately for children learning English, they also have to memorize exceptions to the rule as special cases. Errors with irregular verb forms, especially for infrequently used verbs, can persist well into the school years. It has been widely observed that in the early stages children sometimes produce these irregular pasts seemingly correctly: *I fell*; *It broke*. Then after a while they start saying *I falled*; *It breaked*. At this point we have evidence that they have constructed a rule. They could not be simply learning by imitation because adults do not use these forms. Once children have constructed this rule, they often apply it to every verb they use. They OVERGENERALIZE. Earlier, when they used forms like *I fell* and *I fall*, they probably observed that these were alternative forms for the action of falling, but it is not clear that they realized the significance of that change in form. As their experience grows, they notice that *fall*/*fell* have the same meaning relationship as *call*/*called*. At this point overgeneralization falls away and the irregular past forms reappear.

Past tense

Word formation

Suffix

Overgeneralize

✏ **EXERCISE**

7.2 Analyse this data from a 3-year-old. What rule is he applying? What errors has he made? His pronunciation is given in square brackets.

    a. I like mouses. [mous*iz*]
    b. Leave my feets alone! [feet*s*]
    c. Look at those mans marching. [man*z*]

d. I put three drops. [drop*s*]
e. Gimme those cans. [can*z*]
f. You hurt my foots. [foot*s*]
g. What big horses! [hors*iz*]
h. Funny footses. [foots*iz*]
i. We got prizes. [priz*iz*]

Comment
Plural

This child seems to have grasped the idea of how to form PLURAL nouns: to indicate *more than one*, add an **s** or **z** sound to the end of the word unless it already ends in an **s** or **z** sound, in which case use **iz**. In **a.** and **c.** he is clearly applying this rule. Now all he needs to do is learn about *mice* and *men*. We can also see that he has a foot problem in more ways than one. Not yet sure of the relationship between *foot* and *feet*, he experiments. In **f.** he adds s to foot. In **b.** he adds it to *feet*. And in **h.** he adds an **s** to *foot* and then adds **iz** becauses *foots* ends in an **s**. These sorts of errors involving the overgeneralization of word-formation rules are very common in early childhood. The baby-talk word *footsies* for *feet* is probably a reflection of this.

EXERCISE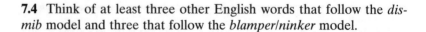

7.3 Here are some more words you have never seen before. In each case try to give a definition of the italicized word.

a. I blamp things all the time. I'm a *blamper*.
b. I need to nink this. Where's the *ninker*?
c. First I mibbed it. Then I *dismibbed* it.

Comment

Even without knowing what *blamp*, *nink* and *mib* mean, you probably got quite far with your definitions. A *blamper* is someone who carries out the action of *blamping*. A *ninker* is a tool or instrument for carrying out the action of *ninking*. And *dismibbing* is the opposite action to *mibbing*. Again, you started learning about this sort of word-formation process in early childhood.

EXERCISE

7.4 Think of at least three other English words that follow the *dis-mib* model and three that follow the *blamper/ninker* model.

Comment

Disappear, disapprove, disagree, and *sitter, runner, computer* are just a few that you could have mentioned. With the past tense ending *-ed* and the plural ending -*s*, we were looking at suffixes which change or add to the base word's meaning in a very limited way. The difference between *drop/dropped* is only a question of whether it happened in the past. The basic action remains the same. Likewise in *cat/cats*, the difference is only one of quantity, not quality. We can describe *drop/dropped* and *cat/cats* as two different forms of the same basic word. In this exercise and the previous one, we see two new detachable elements – the suffix -*er* and the PREFIX *dis*-. But this time we notice that in adding them we have formed **new words**. The action of *disappearing* is quite different from the action of *appearing*. The verb *to run* refers to an action while the noun *runner* refers to the agent of that action. The verb *compute* refers to an action, while the noun *computer* refers to an instrument for carrying out that action.

Prefix

English has a large number of prefixes and suffixes for forming new words: *wash**able**, **re**take, sad**ness**, **in**sane*, are just a few examples. All languages change and adapt to the needs of their speakers. When new words are needed, it is extremely handy to be able to construct them out of existing words by using predictable processes that are recognized and accepted by the speakers of the language. Children as young as 2½ already show a surprising awareness of these processes and can be quite inventive, even more so than adults. This is partly because their vocabularies are still growing. They might not yet know the existing word for the concept they are trying to express, or they may momentarily forget words as in the case of one little girl who referred to her bed as her *sleeper* and then immediately corrected herself.

So far, we have looked at two processes for coining new words – suffixing and prefixing. In this last exercise we turn to some child data to look at two more word-coining processes.

✎ **EXERCISE**

7.5 I have grouped these children's inventions into three broad categories. How would you characterize the process used in each case? The children's ages are given in years and months and the translations/contexts in brackets.

> I. a. 2;0   plate-egg; cup-egg (fried egg; boiled egg)
>   b. 3;0   rat-man (experimental psychologist)
>   c. 3;0   rip-boy . . . no ripper (someone who rips things)
>
> II. a. 2;4   You have to scale it. (weigh cheese)
>   b. 3;11 I'm going to earth this. (bury)
>   c. 2;4   I'm souping. (eating soup)
>
> III. a. 2;6   I'm darking the sky. (colouring a picture)
>   b. 3;0   How do you sharp this? (holding pencil)
>   c. 3;0   Full this up. (holding out a cup)

Comment

Compounding

I Notice that in suffixing and prefixing, elements that are not words on their own are added to whole words. Here both the elements being combined are words in their own right. This process is called COMPOUNDING and is widely used in English. *Batman*, *skinhead*, *windmill* are just a few examples. We can analyse compounds in terms of the word classes being combined and the meaning relationship between them. For example:

> a. *plate-egg* = noun + noun = egg served on a plate
> b. *rip-boy* = verb + noun = boy who rips
> c. *rat-man* = noun + noun = man who works with rats

The child in **b.** was one of the children studied by Clark and Hecht (1982). He was answering the question *What do you call someone who rips things?* His initial choice was a compound word, but he then changed his mind and opted to use the suffix *-er* instead, producing *ripper*.

Conversion

II Here the children have simply **converted** nouns into verbs. In each case the new verb refers to an action associated with a noun involved in that action. CONVERSION is a very productive word-coining process in English and has been used to form verbs which bear a variety of relationships to the original noun. Three of these relationships are reflected in the data. I have also included an existing English word formed on the same basis in brackets:

> a. *to scale* from instrument involved in the action (the verb to fan means to *use a fan*);
> b. *to earth* from location of the action (the verb *to box* can mean *put into a box*);
> c. *to soup* from something moved or affected by the action (the verb *to fish* means to *catch fish*).

Notice that in both **a.** and **b.** the children have produced words that already exist in English, but these words have rather different meanings from the ones the children have intended. The child in **c.** has produced quite a useful word. There is no existing verb in English that specifically means *to eat soup*.

III This is another type of conversion which is fairly common in English. Here, adjectives are directly converted into verbs meaning *to make or become*. Existing examples are: *to slim* meaning to *make or become slim*; *to green* meaning *to make or become green*; *to empty* meaning *to make or become empty*. Notice that in each of these child cases, there are existing English verbs which have the same meaning: *to darken*; *to sharpen*; *to fill*.

   In this unit we have been looking at children mastering the structure of words rather than sentences, but we have seen the same ingenuity and active experimentation that characterize all aspects of language acquisition.

From the two-word stage onwards children start to acquire some of the rules for adapting words to different sentence structures, most notably in English, tense endings on verbs and plural endings on nouns.

Errors like *putted* and *feets* are called overgeneralizations and indicate that children have started to construct a rule system for forming past tenses and plurals rather than simply imitating what they hear.

From the age of 2½, children also start to learn and apply the processes available in their language for coining new words. Compounding and conversion are among the earliest processes that English-speaking children acquire.

 **FURTHER
EXERCISES**

7.6 a. Give three examples of English agent nouns (those which refer to the do-er of the action) formed by adding the suffix *-er* to to a verb.

   b. In **Corpus V** find two instances of children forming nouns in this way.

   c. Which of these two inventions is more likely to be corrected by an adult and why?

   d. In one of the two Dialogues, the child also uses *-er* to form another type of word. Explain this word-formation process. Then find an instance in **Corpus II** where Sophie may well be using the same process.

7.7 a. What word-formation process are the children using for their 'inventions' in **Corpus V:10** and **14**?

   b. In each case think of three existing English words formed on the same basis.

   c. In one of the cases, there is an existing English word which expresses the same concept as the invented word. What is it?

7.8 Analyse the word-coining process used by the child in **Corpus V:12**. Give examples of three existing English words formed on the same basis.

7.9 Find an instance in **Corpus II** where Sophie has overgeneralized the rule used to mark possessor in noun phrase, as in *Annie's ball*. What is wrong with her application of this rule?

7.10 a. In **Corpus I:20**, the child is using an unusual verb form to express past action (for a child of that age). What might be the basis of her choice?

b. Looking at **Corpora II–IV**, who is most likely to have used that form – Sophie, Alison or Kathryn?

7.11 a. Using **Corpus V**, find an instance where the child is coining a new word by compounding.

b. State the **word class** of each of the combined words and the meaning relation between them. (See **Exercise 7.5**.)

c. Think of at least three other English words which are formed on this basis.

d. What is 'wrong' with the child's invention?

7.12 Analyse the error in **Corpus V:8** in terms of what it reveals about how much the child **already knows** about the word-coining process he has used.

7.13 Using **Corpora II–V**, find all the cases where the children have overgeneralized their use of the verb ending -*ed*. In each case explain why the child's choice is an error.

7.14 In **Corpus II:7**, Sophie correctly uses an irregular past tense.

a. Judging from her other dialogues at the same age, can we be sure that she realizes the difference between *break* and *broke*?

b. In **Corpus IV: 2**, Kathryn also correctly uses an irregular past tense form. What evidence do we have that she realizes the difference between *come* and *came*?

7.15 Find an instance in **Corpus II** where Sophie has overgeneralized the rule for forming plural nouns. What is wrong with her application of the rule?

7.16 a. Consider: *uncover, unzip, untie*. How does the prefix *un-* change the meaning of the verbs to which it is attached?

b. Find three instances in **Corpus V** where the children have creatively used this prefix.

c. In one of these instances the child has created a novel word using this prefix plus another word-coining process. What is the other process? (Hint: see **Exercise 7.5**.)

7.17 In this unit we have not discussed the acquisition of the *-ing* verb ending. This is one of the first endings to appear in children's spontaneous speech, and the first verb ending that eventually appears on all occasions where it is required. Can you think of some possible reasons why the *-ing* ending might be acquired before the *-ed* ending?

7.18 Using **Corpus VI:1–9**, is there any evidence that Hannah has begun to mark plurals and to add tense endings to verbs? Can you find any instances where an adult would have used plural or tense marking, but Hannah fails to do so?

8 HAVING A CONVERSATION

We look at some of the features of child-directed language and at some of the ways children's conversational skills develop as they learn to take account of the information needs of their listeners and to make and interpret indirect requests.

If you listen carefully to conversations between adults you will notice that they often refer to people or things which are not actually present in the room. More often than not, they discuss events that have already occurred or ones that have not even happened yet. If they already know which objects or things they are talking about, they use pronouns rather than the actual name of the person or word for the object. They can use quite long and complicated sentences. Their conversation moves forward fairly quickly with few repetitions of what has just been said. They speak rapidly and often do not pronounce all their words distinctly.

Children acquiring language from scratch would not have a very easy time of it if all the 'evidence' for their investigations were like that. But is all their evidence like that? Turn to **Corpus III** and look at **Dialogues 2**, **4** and **6** where we see Alison at 1 year 4 months, 2 years 4 months and 2 years 10 months in conversation with her mother. What do we notice about the language her mother uses?

First of all the length of the mother's sentences tends to be quite similar to the length of Alison's sentences at each point in her development. The complexity of the mother's sentences also tends to increase as the child gets older. If you look at the last two sentence pairs in **Dialogue 2** and cover the M/C notation it is quite impossible to tell who is who. Now compare these to her mother's opening lines in **Dialogue 6**: *maybe he'd like to see the truck*. Again, if we cover up the M/C notation it is hard to tell who is who.

We notice that the mother sometimes repeats the child's utterance, expanding it into a more complete version:

C: juice.
M: *shall we have some* juice?

C: I want try that—that necklace.
M: You want *to* try this necklace?

The mother sometimes takes one or two of the same words used by the child and uses them in a slightly different sentence structure:

C: I think he'll play *with the truck.* (preposition + noun phrase)
M: Yes. I think he *likes the truck.* (verb + noun phrase).

Another variation on this, although not as clearly demonstrated in these dialogues, is to repeat the same sentence structure with substitutions in one of the grammatical 'slots'. Here a mother makes a series of substitutions in the subject slot and in her final sentence she also substitutes an expanded noun phrase into the object slot:

C: Mummy making cake.
M: And Baby's making cake. And Sissy's making cake. We're making very nice cakes.

We also notice that the mother tends to use pronouns less often than we would expect. Given the previous context it would seem more natural to say to an adult or older child:

Shall we have some? (some juice)
You want to try it? (this necklace)
I think he likes it. (the truck)

In the earliest dialogue we see that the mother even refrains from using *me* and *you*, referring to herself as *Mommy* and the child as *Baby*. This happens more frequently when children are in the one-word and two-word stages.

When the child has difficulties choosing the right word, the mother supplies the appropriate one, explicitly calling the child's attention to the new word: *You know what this is called? See, it's a microphone.* Parents do not do this on every occasion. They sometimes ignore inappropriate vocabulary, especially if the child has more or less got the idea across. But they rarely call attention to grammatical errors in an explicit way. In the dialogue here, rather than saying: *Do you know how to say that? Listen. You say, 'I want TO try this necklace'.* the mother simply repeats the construction in her own sentence adding the *to*. Research by Shatz (1982) has shown that only about 4 per cent of all children's errors are explicitly corrected by parents and the overwhelming majority of these are vocabulary errors.

One reason for this is that in the early stages parents often work very hard to keep the conversation flowing. Have you noticed how often in the Corpus, the mother states the obvious and asks the child questions to which she already knows the answer? Children make so many grammatical errors while they are learning (often two or three in a single sentence if they are trying something complicated) that conversations would break down entirely under the strain of grammar lessons.

Another reason is that children are quite receptive to being given new words to add to their vocabulary, and will often ask for help in this area. However they tend to be very **unreceptive** to being 'taught' points of grammar. They seem to prefer working the rules out for themselves. They usually ignore explicit corrections or miss the point entirely. **Dialogue 9** in **Corpus V** provides a graphic and typical example. Here is a further example from a 6-year-old:

> C: Who do you think is the importantest kid in the world?
> M: What did you say Jamie?
> C: Who do you think is the specialest kid in the world?

What prompted Jamie to rephrase his remark, and incidentally repeat the same error with a different word? He seems to have interpreted his mother's question as indicating that his effort at communication was not entirely successful. So he tries again. This process works both ways. A 'What?' question from the child who has clearly heard what was said often prompts the adult to rephrase, using simpler vocabulary or sentence structure.

Although *See, it's a microphone* is the only example in these three dialogues, adults also tend to use more exclamations like *See!*, *Look!* and *Oh!* when speaking to children and they tend address them by name as in: *Jamie, Grandma's coming today*; *We'll sit here, Adam*. These sorts of devices command the children's attention and let them know that out of all the surrounding chatter, this particular piece of language is directed to them.

When you do the exercises at the end of this unit you will see, if you have not noticed already, that the language directed to Sophie and Kathryn is very similar to that directed to Alison. Unfortunately, what the Corpus cannot give you is an idea of what the adults' speech actually sounds like. This is why, if at all possible, you should try one of the projects associated with this unit which you will find in **Unit 11** 'Exploring Children's Language'. If you do so, you will probably observe several distinguishing features in the way CHILD-DIRECTED LANGUAGE sounds.

Child-directed language

1 Adults tend to use a higher pitch when speaking to young children.
2 They tend to pause more often, particularly between sentence units, and to speak more slowly.
3 They tend to pronounce their words more clearly and distinctly.
4 They tend to use an exaggerated intonation. For example, they emphasize some words in the sentence far more than they would with adults, or use a very prominent 'rising' tone to distinguish questions from statements.

An important point to remember, though, is that some cultures use very little child-directed language, and even those parents who do tend to simplify and clarify their language for young children do not always do this. From the very beginning, parents' speech to children contains a whole range of different sentence structures and sometimes they talk to their children in a very adult manner. It seems that this is just as important for successful language acquisition as are the simplifications. Nor do parents always restrict their responses to rephrasings or expansions of the child's utterances. If they did, conversations with their children would never get anywhere. It is quite important for conversations between children and adults 'to get somewhere' because becoming a fully-fledged speaker of a language does not simply involve knowing what the words mean and how to construct different types of sentences. It also involves learning the art of conversation.

The early conversations in the Corpus seem very tied to the 'here and now' while the later conversations branch out into discussions of past or future events and even imaginary events. You will also have noticed that successful interpretation of children's early utterances is very dependent on the adults already knowing what is going on both in the situation and in the child's head.

As children's conversations move away from discussing the immediate situation and as they gain greater experience in talking to people who do not know them as well as their parents do, their use of language begins to take into account just how much information their listener knows or can infer and how much they as speakers need to provide.

Part of their progress stems from general intellectual development – an increased capacity to remember and interpret past events, the ability to conceive of and plan for events that are still only possibilities, and the realization that other people do not necessarily share their own perspective or knowledge. And of course, part of their progress stems from their acquisition of the linguistic skills necessary for providing their listeners with this knowledge. The ability to use auxiliary verbs and verb endings to indicate whether or not an event happened in the past, is ongoing, or only a possibility is one example of this. But there are some more subtle linguistic conventions that often take quite a while to sort out.

1 The appropriate use of the articles *a* and *the*. *The* is generally reserved for use when **both** speaker and listener know what is being referred to. For example: *Annie saw **a frog** in her pond. She tried to put **the frog** into **a jar**. But **the jar** was too small.* Try reversing the order of use of *a/the* in each case to see what the inappropriate use sounds like.

2 The appropriate use of pronouns. This can be quite tricky, because it seems much more natural in a conversation to use pronouns rather than repeatedly using the original phrase. On the other hand, it must be clear to both speaker and listener what the pronouns are referring

to. Try reversing the order of use of *Annie* and *she* in the sentence above or replacing *a frog*, *a jar* and *the jar* with *it* in a variety of combinations and you will see what I mean.

Indirect request

3 INDIRECT REQUESTS. Making a request can be done in such a way that no one can misunderstand you: *Give me some candy please*; or *I want some candy*. But this can sound a bit abrupt or even unfriendly. On the other hand, people might find it more polite and perhaps comply more readily if you took a more subtle approach and asked a question as one 4-year-old did: *I wonder if we have any candy in the house?* Sometimes children overdo this as did the even older child who said: *Do you possibly have any water that I could drink?* Children also take some time to learn how to understand indirect requests. Have you ever had your phone call answered by a toddler who interpreted your indirect request for action as a simple request for information?

A: Hi Toby, this is Uncle Jack. Is your mum home?
C: Yes. (followed by silence)
A: Can I talk to her?
C: Yes. (followed by silence)
A: Please call her, will you?
C: Oh. Okay.

UNIT SUMMARY

In many cultures, adults, especially caregivers, use a style of speech to young children known as child-directed language which tends to be simpler and clearer than that used with other adults or older children.

Competent speakers need to know not only the vocabulary and grammar of their language but also how to carry out a socially appropriate conversation.

Two of the areas where children make considerable conversational progress during their first five years are learning how to take into account how much their hearer already knows and how to make and interpret polite requests.

FURTHER EXERCISES

8.1 Given the general lack of verb endings and auxiliary verbs, children's early sentences can often have a variety of possible interpretations and expansions. For example, *Daddy jump* could mean *Daddy is jumping* (ongoing); *Daddy jumped* (past); *Daddy can jump* (possibility). Without looking at the dialogue, write three possible expansions for Sophie's first sentence in **Corpus II:2**: *you take a bissy*. Then look at the dialogue. Which one of these interpretations did her mother choose?

8.2 a. Find four instances in **Corpus II** where the mother's response repairs but does not explictly correct an error involving verb or noun endings in Sophie's previous utterance.

b. Find three instances in **Corpus II** where the response of Sophie's mother repairs the omission of an auxiliary verb.

8.3 a. In **Corpus II:1–10**, what is Sophie's usual way of asking her mother for something?

b. In **Corpus II:20–26**, find five examples of Sophie making indirect requests.

c. What indirect request does Kathryn make in **Corpus IV:4**?

8.4 Find three instances in **Corpus II:1–10** where Sophie's mother repeats the child's error in her own response **without** repairing it. State the error in each case.

8.5 Using the same procedure you followed in **Exercise 8.1**, write expansions for *Daddy come down too* in **Corpus II:3**. Which interpretation did her mother choose? Is that what Sophie meant?

8.6 a. Using **Corpus II, IV, V**, find four instances where a question or obvious misunderstanding from the adult prompts the children to attempt to repair or rephrase their previous utterance.

b. Find the instance in **Corpus II** where Sophie's query results in her mother rephrasing her previous sentence into a simpler one.

8.7 a. Analyse Sophie's error in the use of *a/the* in **Corpus II:15**.
b. Is her use appropriate in **Corpus II:24**?

8.8 Using **Corpus II:24**, find an instance where Sophie's pronoun use is potentially confusing to the listener. Why?

8.9 Discuss the ways in which dialogues **III:5** and **IV:1** illustrate common features of child-directed language.

✐ **SUPPLE-MENTARY EXERCISES**

Contingent response

8.10 In adult conversations each speaker tends to respond in some relevant way to what the previous speaker said. This is known as making a CONTINGENT RESPONSE. If their response is **not** going to be relevant to the current topic, speakers usually signal to their listener that they are going to 'change the subject'. Analyse the conversations in **Corpus II:19, 20** and **Corpus VI:6, 7, 10, 12** in terms of contingent or non-contingent responses and possible reasons for the non-contingent responses.

8.11 Discuss the ways these 7-year-old children use pronouns and articles in their written descriptions of a wooden horse.

1 On the wooden horse it has blue shiny paint. It has a muzzle round its face and it has a cross in yellow on its tummy. It feels smooth with a pointy ear and has a rabbit tail. Its eyes and nose are just three dots and it has a curly mane. He is podgy and his legs are little.

2 It came from Sweden. It's got the Swedish flag on it. It's made from wood. It's painted in the following colours: white, dark blue and yellow. It is quite smooth but bumpy in places. You can almost see the grain on the hooves. It is a wooden horse.

8.12 In **Corpus VI:1–13**, do you think that Hannah's babysitter uses child-directed language? Why?

8.13 In **Corpus VI:1–13**, what form do Hannah's requests usually take? Did you find any instances of Hannah making **indirect** requests?

8.14 Choose your own examples from **Corpora V** and **VI** to support your answer to the following question. Does the correction of children's errors by adults play an important role in language acquisition?

LEARNING TO GET
THE SOUNDS RIGHT

9

We introduce the study of children's acquisition of the sound system of their language and look at children's early pronunciations which involve the deletion or addition of certain sounds.

Up until now we have been primarily looking at how children use words and how they structure them into sentences. Here we concentrate on what their words actually sound like. In order to begin our study of children's acquisition of the sound system, or PHONOLOGY, of their language we need to make a distinction between two types of sounds, VOWELS and CONSONANTS. In written language various combinations of **a**, **e**, **i**, **o**, **u** (and sometimes **y**) usually represent the vowel sounds. If you say the following words out loud you will notice that the sounds in bold, the vowels, are made with virtually no obstruction to the air flow. The other sounds in these words, the consonants, all involve some degree of momentary obstruction to the air flow:

Phonology

Vowel
Consonant

    y**a**k b**e**nt d**u**st s**i**ll**y** f**ee**l m**oo**n pl**a**y l**ie** g**o**t

                                                   ✐ **EXERCISE**

9.1 Here are some representative examples of a child's early words and the adult targets at which she is aiming. How would you characterize the way her pronunciations differ from the adult versions?

	Adult target	*Child's version*
(who)	hu	hu
(cat)	ka**t**	ka
(bib)	bi**b**	bi
(toy)	toi	toi

	Adult target	*Child's version*
(noise)	noi**z**	noi
(back)	ba**k**	ba
(loo)	lu	lu

Comment

You will have noticed that where an adult word ends in a consonant sound, the child is deleting this final sound in her own productions. This is quite a common tendency in early speech, especially in the beginning stages.

You will also have noticed the rather odd spelling which I have used. If you go on to read slightly more advanced books on child phonology, you will find that children's speech is usually transcribed in a special international phonetic alphabet which can give a much more exact and less ambiguous recreation of the child's pronunciation. When studying phonology, we must be very careful not to confuse actual speech sounds with their written expression. In English there is not always a one-to-one correspondence between a letter (or letters) and the sound being symbolized. In this book we will be using a very simplified type of phonetic alphabet for the transcription of some speech sounds to help avoid this confusion.

The example below illustrates how a more phonetic spelling can capture similarities and differences between consonant sounds that can be masked by ordinary spelling. All the segments in **bold** in each group represent the same sounds. Say each word aloud to yourself to verify this.

a. **qu**it **k**ick **sc**holar **c**od : **kw**it **k**ik **sk**olar **k**od
b. **z**oo re**s**in slam**s** : **z**u re**z**in slam**z**
c. cou**gh** cof**f**in **ph**ysics : ko**f** ko**f**in **f**iziks
d. **m**ap la**mb** bu**m**p : **m**ap la**m** bu**m**p
e. **c**ell **s**ent cat**s** blit**z** : **s**el **s**ent kat**s** blit**s**
f. bun**i**on **y**acht **y**early : bun**y**on **y**ot **y**earli
g. **wh**ack **qu**ickly went : **w**ak **kw**ikli went

EXERCISE ✎

9.2 Try this exercise to get yourself used to thinking in terms of sounds rather than standard spellings. Rewrite the following words to reflect the *sounds* of the segments in **bold**:

a. **kn**ot
b. du**ck**
c. yam**s**
d. hat**s**
e. lau**gh**
f. du**mb**
g. **c**an
h. **c**entral
i. on**i**on
j. **wh**o
k. **wh**en
l. **qu**est

Your 'rewrites' should look something like this:

a. **n**ot   e. la**f**   i. on**y**on
b. du**k**   f. du**m**   j. **h**u
c. yam**z**   g. ka**n**   k. **w**en
d. hat**s**   h. **s**entral   l. k**w**est

Don't be discouraged if you found this task rather difficult at first. We are so used to thinking of words in terms of their written form that it often takes a bit of time to start thinking of them in terms of their actual sounds again. I say 'again' because, in some ways, studying the acquisition of phonology involves a return to our early childhood. When you were a year old and learning the sound system of your language, you had no access to the written form of words. You were operating only on the speech sounds you heard around you. As you work through the exercises in this unit and the next, you should find this task easier.

9.3 We shall return now to another common feature of children's pronunciation patterns. How would you characterize the deviations from the adult targets which this child is making?

	Adult target	Child's version
(ask)	ask	ak
(glue)	glu	gu
(plastic)	plastik	patik
(strap)	strap	tap

In common with many other languages, English has quite a few words where consonant sounds occur in clusters; *ask*, *glue*, *plastic* and *strap* are just four examples. Have you noticed that in each case the child has simplified, or reduced, these clusters by deleting one or more of their consonants?

9.4 Look at the following data from a variety of children. What type of **substitution** or **addition** characterizes these children's pronunciations? In this exercise we introduce a new sound symbol ə. This vowel is the sound of the final **a** in *vanilla*.

	Adult target	Child's version
(egg)	eg	egə
(pig)	pig	pigə
(blue)	blu	bəlu
(button)	butn	butu
(apple)	apl	apo

Comment

Each of these cases involves either the substitution of a consonant sound by a vowel sound or the addition of an extra vowel to the word. In *egg* and *pig*, the vowel sound has been added to the end of the word after the final consonant. In *blue* the vowel has been inserted in the consonant cluster **bl**. With *button* and *apple*, a vowel has been **substituted** for the final consonant sound. In English, most syllables contain a vowel sound. But sometimes the consonants **n** and **l** can form a syllable on their own, especially at the ends of words. This is also true of the consonant sound **r** in American English and some varieties of British English. It is quite common for children, especially **Syllabic consonant**   those acquiring English, to replace these SYLLABIC CONSONANTS with vowels.

So far we have looked at three common and systematic deviations that young children tend to make in their early pronunciations: deletion of final consonants, cluster reduction and the addition/substitution of vowel sounds. These might seem to be quite different processes, but if we look at them from a slightly different perspective, perhaps we can find a unifying factor.

EXERCISE ✎

9.5 In this set we return to four of the adult/child word pairs from our previous examples:

	Adult target	Child's version
(blue)	blu	bəlu
(glue)	glu	gu
(pig)	pig	pigə
(bib)	bib	bi

Each of these words contains both consonants and vowels in a particular order. We can make consonant/vowel (C/V) diagrams for each of these words using the phonetic versions to make sure that we are paying attention to actual speech sounds. Let's try doing this for *blue*.

Adult target	Child's version
CCV (blu)	CVCV (bəlu)

Now, try making C/V diagrams for the remaining 3 word pairs: *glue*, *pig* and *bib*.

Comment

Your C/V diagrams should look like this:

Adult target	Child's version
CCV (glu)	CV (gu)
CVC (pig)	CVCV (pigə)
CVC (bib)	CV (bi)

In the process of making and comparing these diagrams, have you noticed that the children seem to be expressing a preference for word structures characterized by simple alternations of consonants and vowels? This preference has been noted in children acquiring a variety of languages, not just English. They often restructure adult pronunciations to fit in with this preferred CVCV pattern. We must emphasize, however, that while this is a general tendency, children do not necessarily restructure or simplify all their words in this way. Notice than in **Exercise 9.3**, despite the various cluster reductions, all the word-final consonants were pronounced.

Complete deletion of a final consonant is a relatively early process. Children can often cope with one final consonant fairly quickly, and eventually they can cope with two or more consonants in clusters as well. Children also vary in the degree to which they find certain consonant and vowel patterns difficult to pronounce, and even individual children find some consonants easier to pronounce in one context than another. Neil Smith, a linguist who made a detailed study of his own child's early pronunciation patterns (1973), found that his son deleted **m** when it clustered with **p** at the ends of words but had no trouble when it occurred on its own. At the same age (2 years 2 months) his son pronounced *bump* as *bup* but *room* was correctly pronounced.

✏ **EXERCISE**

9.6 So far we have been talking about deletions which have involved restructuring the consonant/vowel patterns of words. Take a look at this data from a child between the ages of 2½ and 3½. Can we make some sort of generalization about the elements which he is deleting?

	Adult target	*Child's version*	*Age*
(behind)	be–'hind	hind	2;5
(supposed)	su–'pozd	pozd	2;7
(tomato)	to–'ma – to	ma–to	2;8
(without)	with–'out	out	2;7
(difficult)	'dif–i–kult	dif–kult	3;4

Here, the transcriptions have a bit more detail. All these words are divided into syllables with the STRESSED SYLLABLE marked with '. (The stressed syllable of a word is the one that tends to be pronounced more loudly than the rest.) With this extra information we can start to make some generalizations about the child's deletions. First we notice that in these words of two or more syllables, the child is deleting whole syllables, not just single consonants. Now let's see if there seems to be any logic underlying the choice of syllable to be deleted. You will notice that in each case the child has deleted an **unstressed** syllable. Again, this reflects a general tendency in early speech, regardless of the particular language which the child is acquiring.

Comment
Stressed syllable

In the next unit we will move on to some rather more challenging problems in the analysis of early speech patterns. For now, the following exercises will give you a chance to practise the kinds of linguistic analysis that we have used so far.

UNIT SUMMARY

Children's early deviations from adult pronunciation often show a definite pattern and can be described as processes.

Final consonant omission, consonant cluster reduction, addition of a vowel between consonants and at the end of a word, and substitution of a vowel for a syllabic consonant all help to produce words with a CVCV sound structure, which very young children tend to prefer.

In words of more than one syllable, children often omit one or more of the unstressed syllables.

FURTHER EXERCISES ✎

9.7 a. Find two examples of cluster reduction in **Corpus II**. Transcribe both the target and the child's version into a phonetic spelling and state which consonant has been deleted in each case.
   b. Use **Corpus II:6–8** to find five examples of consonant clusters correctly pronounced.

9.8 a. **Corpus I:18–20** are from the same child. In each case transcribe the target, compare it to the child's version and state what phonological process is involved.
   b. Predict the child's version of *cotton* and *bottle*.

9.9 a. Using **Corpus II**, find two examples of final consonant deletion and state the deleted consonant.
   b. Find six examples of **syllable** deletion.

9.10 a. Using **Corpus I:21–26**, transcribe the targets and compare them to the children's versions.
   b. Make C/V diagrams of both versions.
   c. Identify the type or types of phonological simplifications made in each case.

9.11 Many languages have standard 'baby-talk' words which are often used when speaking to young children. These tend to reflect the kinds of sound simplification processes that children use themselves. Below are some examples from English and Comanche (an American Indian language).

a. For each word state the process or processes involved in producing the baby-talk version.

b. Make C/V diagrams of both adult and baby-talk versions for each word. What pattern emerges?

Note: the Comanche words are already in a phonetic transcription.

		Adult	*Baby-talk*
English		1. biscuit	bickie
		2. stomach	tummy
		3. dog	doggie
Comanche		4. mupik ('owl')	mupi
		5. tatoko ('toe')	tato
		6. kwana ('odour')	pana

The Comanche data is from Casagrande (1964).

 **SUPPLE-MENTARY EXERCISES**

9.12 We have noted that speech sounds can be put into two major classes, **consonants** and **vowels**. Five-year-old Nico has just begun to learn how to write. Here are some samples from one of his stories with 'translations' in brackets Which class of sound does he tend to omit in his writing?

> *I ws tcn by a ailn* (I was taken by an alien)
> *thn mummy sd we hfto go in 1 [one] of thy rockets* (then mummy said we have to go in one of the rockets)

9.13 In **Corpus VI:1–13**, find all the instances of **consonant cluster reduction**. Does there appear to be any pattern which predicts which consonant will be retained and which one or ones will be omitted?

9.14 In **Corpus VII:1**, find all the instances of **final consonant deletion**. Does the child still do this in **VII:2** where she is three months older?

9.15 In **Corpora VI** and **VII**, find the instances of **syllable deletion**. Are there any instances where the **stressed** syllable has been deleted?

9.16 Using **Corpus VII:1** make C/V diagrams of the adult targets and of the child's pronunciations as you did in **Exercise 9.5**. Do they confirm young children's preference for CVCV sound patterns?

10 STILL LEARNING: 'DOGS' AND 'GOGS'

> We analyse some of the more complex patterns in children's speech. To explain these patterns we introduce the analysis of consonant sounds by their manner and place of articulation and their voicing.

EXERCISE ✎

10.1 Here are some examples of young children's words and their adult forms from a variety of languages. In what way do the deviations in this sample differ from those we have been looking at in **Unit 9**?

Adult target	Child's version	Language
sundar	**t**undar	Hindi
hu**s**	hu**t**	Norwegian
zebra	**d**ebra	English
fazik	**p**azik	Hungarian
sopa	**t**opa	Spanish

Comment

Here, we see that the children have substituted one consonant sound with another one rather than deleting it altogether or replacing it with a vowel sound. In this sample the particular choice of the replacement is not a random one. But to understand this pattern, we have to make some distinctions between consonants. One of these distinctions is their MANNER OF ARTICULATION. The consonants **b**, **p**, **d**, **t** are STOP consonants. In making them the airflow is momentarily completely blocked, resulting in a 'popping' sound when they are released. The consonants **v**, **f**, **z**, **s** are FRICATIVE consonants. In making these consonants the airflow is only partially blocked, resulting in air friction which produces a 'hissing' noise as they are being pronounced. Now, if we apply this distinction to our sample,

Manner of articulation
Stop

Fricative

68

you can see that in each case the fricative consonants in the adult targets have been replaced by stop consonants.

So, we have solved half of the puzzle. But how do we explain the particular choice of the stop consonant replacement? We see that **t** consistently replaces **s**, for example. But **t** is only one of the possible choices of stop consonants. To help explain this half of the puzzle, we need to make a further distinction between consonants, their PLACE OF ARTICULATION, the place in the mouth where the airflow is obstructed. Try saying *pan* and *fan* aloud slowly and carefully. You will notice that in both cases the airflow is obstructed at the lips. But while the **p** produces the characteristic 'popping' sound of stops, **f** produces the 'hissing' sound of fricatives. You will notice the same distinction when you say *bat* and *vat*. Like **p** and **f**, **b** and **v** are LABIAL consonants. Now try saying *tin* and *sin*, paying particular attention to where your tongue forms an obstruction to the airflow. You will notice that in both cases the airflow is obstructed on the area just behind your upper front teeth, the ALVEOLAR RIDGE. But again, the **t** produces a 'popping' sound while **s** produces a 'hissing' one. We notice the same distinction when we say *dip* and *zip*. **Table 10.1** lets us summarize the distinctions we have made between these consonant sounds in terms of their place and manner of articulation.

Place of articulation

Labial

Alveolar ridge

Table 10.1 Place and manner of articulation for the sounds **b, p, d, t, v, f, z, s**

	Place of Articulation		
	Labial	*Alveolar*	
Manner of Articulation			
Stops	**b** **p**	**d** **t**	
Fricatives	**v** **f**	**z** **s**	

We can now make a further generalization about the STOPPING PROCESS. Children tend to replace fricatives with stop consonants which have the same place of articulation.

Stopping process

✎ **EXERCISE**

10.2 Here is a more complicated puzzle. We have seen that **d** and **t** are both stops, and that **s** and **z** are both fricatives. We have also seen that all four of these consonants have their place of articulation at the alveolar ridge. Look at the following data from a 2-year-old child. How can we account for the fact that the child consistently replaces **s** with **t** and **z** with **d**?

	Adult target	Child's version
(zip)	zip	dip
(fuzz)	fuz	fud
(sip)	sip	tip
(miss)	mis	mit

Comment
Voicing Voiced

Voiceless

To do this, we need to make a third distinction between consonants, their VOICING. Some consonants are VOICED, that is the vocal cords are vibrating while they are being pronounced, producing a 'buzzing' sound. Other consonants are VOICELESS, made without vocal cord vibration, producing a 'whispering' sound. Consonants which have the same place and manner of articulation can still differ as to whether or not they are voiced. Try saying the following word pairs aloud slowly and carefully:

bat/**p**at **d**ug/**t**ug **v**an/**f**an **z**ip/**s**ip

Can you hear the difference in voicing between **b/p**; **d/t**; **v/f**; **z/s**?

Now, if we apply this voiced/voiceless contrast to the child's speech in **Exercise 10.2**, we can see that in each case, although the child has replaced a fricative with a stop consonant, he has chosen a stop consonant with the same place of articulation and the same voicing. This is a common characteristic of the stopping process. Look again at the pairs in **Exercise 10.1**. You will notice the same principle at work. Ease of production has a lot to do with the stopping process. Fricatives require a much finer control of the tongue and lips than stops do. Initially, children seem to find it easier to block the airflow completely rather than only partially.

EXERCISE ✎

10.3 Bearing the voiced/voiceless contrast in mind, we turn now to another common substitution process in children's speech. Can you spot a pattern in this child's pronunciation of the following words?

	Adult target	Child's version
(bed)	bed	bet
(bad)	bad	bat
(tub)	tub	dup
(kick)	kik	gik
(pip)	pip	bip
(bag)	bag	bak
(back)	bak	bak

Comment

You will recall from the previous data sets that **b/p** are a voiced/voiceless pair of labial stops and that **d/t** are a voiced/voiceless pair of alveolar stops. There is one more pair of voiced/voiceless stops in English, **g/k**. Try saying *dug* and *duck* (*duk*) slowly and carefully paying particular attention to the position of your tongue when pronouncing the **g** and **k** as well as to whether or not your vocal cords were vibrating. Did you notice that **g** was voiced while **k** was voiceless? Did you notice that in producing both these consonants the airflow was completely obstructed rather far back in your mouth? This area is called the soft palate, or VELUM.

Velum

Armed with this knowledge, we can see that the child in **Exercise 10.3** seems to have a rule that uses the voiced partner of a consonant pair when it is the first sound of a word and the voiceless partner when it is the last sound in a word. This too is a fairly common phenomenon in early speech. Notice that if the child could not hear the voicing difference between pair members, we would expect the consonants to occur in random positions, which they clearly do not.

✏ **EXERCISE**

10.4 Here we encounter a rather fascinating process which children use to simplify adult pronunciation patterns. We also introduce the details of another consonant pair, **m/n**. Try saying *mat* and *bat* aloud slowly and carefully. You will notice that both **b** and **m** involve complete closure of the lips and vibration of the vocal cords. But in pronouncing **m**, the air is allowed to escape through the nose, producing the characteristic 'humming' sound of NASAL consonants. **Nasal** If you try saying *nip* and *dip* you will notice that both **n** and **d** involve closure at the alveolar ridge and that both are voiced. But **n** like **m** has the characteristic nasal hum. Now, look at the following data from several children. How can we account for the kinds of substitutions which they are making?

	Adult target	Child's version
(Sam)	sam	nam
(dock)	dok	gok
(tub)	tub	bub
(dog)	dog	gog

Comment

Children frequently modify consonants to make them more like other consonants in the same word. Usually initial consonants assimilate to later ones, but not always. If we look closely at the data here, we can see this process of ASSIMILATION in action. You will notice that in *dog* **Assimilation** and *tub*, the initial consonant has assimilated completely to the final one. In the other two examples, the assimilation is only partial. In *Sam* the initial **s** has become a nasal under the influence of the final **m** but has kept its alveolar place of articulation resulting in **n**. In *dock* the **d** has become a velar consonant under the influence of the final **k**, but has retained its voiced quality, resulting in its replacement with **g**, the voiced partner of **k**.

Sometimes, children can carry the assimilation process even further in two-syllable words by assimilating whole syllables. Thus *water* becomes *wawa* and *bottle* becomes *baba*. This process is so common in early childhood that this REDUPLICATION OF SYLLABLES has become **Reduplication of** standard in 'baby-talk' . . . *choo-choo* for *train*, *wee-wee* for *urinate*, **syllables** *bye-bye* for *goodbye* are just a few examples.

In this unit we have looked at three more phonological processes used by children: **stopping**, **voicing/de-voicing of consonant sounds**, and **assimilation**. If you go on to further study of children's speech patterns, you will encounter yet others. But in all cases, you will find that a detailed analysis of the sounds involved helps to find seemingly hidden patterns in children's 'mistakes'. One way of thinking about children's acquisition of the sound system of their language is as the dual task of building up a mental picture of how words *should* sound and then trying to put this into practice in actual speech. It is not surprising that along the way children make simplifications which allow them to reduce the number of sounds and contrasts between sounds that they need to pay attention to at any one time. They do this in a variety of ways, as we have seen, and we must bear in mind that there is considerable variation between children in their preferences for particular processes. Nevertheless, I hope that even this brief excursion into child phonology has shown you that in acquiring the sound system of their language, the simplifications which children make are systematic linguistic ones.

Table 10.2 provides a summary of information about the English consonants we have been discussing. You might find it helpful in completing the **Further Exercises** for this unit.

Table 10.2 Voicing, place and manner of articulation for the sounds **b, p, d, t, v, f, z, s, g, k, m, n**

	Place of Articulation					
	Labial		Alveolar		Velar	
	Voiced	*Voiceless*	*Voiced*	*Voiceless*	*Voiced*	*Voiceless*
Manner of Articulation						
Stops	**b**	**p**	**d**	**t**	**g**	**k**
Fricatives	**v**	**f**	**z**	**s**		
Nasals	**m**		**n**			

UNIT SUMMARY

Young children often change the consonants in their words to others which are simpler for them to produce.

These simplification processes include: replacing fricatives with stops, voicing all consonants at the beginning of words, de-voicing all consonants at the ends of words, and either partially or completely assimilating a consonant to another consonant in the same word.

Young children can also assimilate whole syllables to another syllable in the word. This process is called reduplication and can be found in many standard baby talk words.

FURTHER EXERCISES ✎

10.5 A child uses the following pronunciations in *italic*:

kick:*gik* flap:*vlap* cod:*got* have:*haf* toy:*doi*

a. Transcribe the adult targets and compare them to the child's versions. What rule underlies the substitutions?

b. Predict the child's versions of *pig*, *keep* and *bit*.

10.6 Corpus I:1–7 each come from a different child.

a. Transcribe each target word and identify the phonological process involved in each of the child versions.

b. How might **Child 3** pronounce *buzz* and **Child 4** pronounce *top*?

10.7 Corpus I:8–14 come from the same child.

a. Transcribe the target words and identify the phonological process involved here.

b. What principle seems to underlie the child's choice of which consonant to delete?

10.8 Using **Corpus II**, find an example of **consonant addition**. What might have influenced the child's choice of consonant?

10.9 In **Corpus II**, you will find an instance of the **mother** using 'baby-talk'. What phonological processes have been applied to produce the baby-talk version?

10.10 This final exercise is quite challenging. If you can solve these puzzles, you are well on your way to tackling more advanced study in this area. In these units, we have generally been looking at phonological processes in isolation. However, it is very common for more than one process to operate on a single word.

a. Using **Corpus I:15–17**, transcribe the targets and compare them to the children's versions.

b. For each item, state which processes have operated and in what order.

Example:

crab target = ***krab*** child = ***gab***.

1 cluster reduction: **kr** to **k**
2 consonant voicing before a vowel **k** to **g**

🖉 **SUPPLE-MENTARY EXERCISES**

10.11 The sounds **l** and **r**, which are two more voiced consonants, can be quite difficult for young children. Some children use them interchangeably. More commonly, some children replace them with the sound of **y** in *yet* or the sound of **w** in *wet*. These **y** and **w** sounds are

Glide consonants

Gliding

sometimes called GLIDE CONSONANTS and the process of replacing **l** or **r** with them is called GLIDING. Find the instances of gliding in **Corpus VI:10, 11, 12**. How would you characterize the child's pronunciations of *window* and *purple* in **Corpus VII:2**?

10.12 What examples of **initial consonant voicing** and/or **final consonant de-voicing** can you find in **Corpus VII:1**? Compare those examples to the child's pronunciation in **Corpus VII:2**. What changes have occurred, if any?

10.13 A fricative type consonant that we did not cover in this unit is the first sound of *job*. In **Corpus VI:10** find an instance of Hannah **stopping** this consonant.

10.14 Two further fricative consonants are both represented by the letters 'th' in English spelling. One is the first sound of *thin*. This voiceless fricative is made by putting the tongue between the teeth. Its voiced partner is the first sound in *this*. In **Corpus VI** find the instances of **stopping** in Hannah's pronunciations when she encounters these sounds. What other types of sounds does she sometimes substitute for these fricatives?

10.15 Using **Corpus VII**, identify and compare the simplification processes the child uses at ages 2;2 and 2;5 for: *yoghurt, puzzle, piggy, tractor, stroller, apple*. Do you notice any instances where a velar consonant has been replaced with one which is articulated **Fronting** further forward in the mouth. This process is called FRONTING.

EXPLORING CHILDREN'S LANGUAGE: PROJECTS

11

Before you get started on your project, there are some general guidelines which you should follow:

- Whenever you are working with children, make sure that you obtain permission from either their parents or teacher (if you are collecting data in a school).
- Assure the parents or teacher that your investigation is for your own personal study and that neither the identity of the child nor that of the school or family will appear in your report. You can refer to children in your write-up by their first initial or by a pseudonym.
- You should explain the nature of your investigation and emphasize that your goal is not to evaluate individual children in any way but rather to learn about children's language development in general.
- By all means, show the data you have collected to the parents or teacher, but if they ask you for your opinion of the child's progress, you should always answer simply that as far as you know, the child's responses seem quite typical for children of that age.
- Remember that children are people! If they become tired or want to discontinue the activity despite your gentle encouragement, you **must** respect their wishes. You may have to take a break or return at another time to complete your investigation.
- Unless the specific purpose of your project is to observe the child in conversation with other people, you and the child should be alone in a quiet room without parents or other children present. In a nursery school, this will probably be impossible, but choose the quietest corner you can find. The presence of others can be distracting to the child and the extra noise may make the child's responses difficult to record accurately.

- Keep careful records of the date of the session, the child's age at the time, and any other background information which the various projects might require.
- Most of these projects can be carried out by writing down responses and the situations in which they occurred in a notebook, but **if at all possible**, try to tape-record your sessions as well. Tapes will provide you with invaluable information which you might miss or forget to record if you are relying solely on the notebook method.
- When asking children questions which have a right or wrong answer, give no indication to them as to the correctness of their answer. Simply say 'Okay' in a neutral tone of voice after each response. First, you don't want to discourage them, and second, you don't want their subsequent responses to be influenced by your reactions.

UNIT 1

1 Make a survey of children's first words. Find as many parents of young children as you can and ask them what their child's first word was. Explain that this should be the first recognizable word the child spontaneously produced (not a simple imitation). If possible, find out the age (in years and months) when the children produced their first words. Then answer the following questions in relation to your data:

   a. Categorize these first words by their meaning types as in **Exercise 1.1**. Did any meaning type prove to be the most common?
   b. For the words that named things, were there any similarities or differences between children as to the people or objects named?
   c. What was the average age for children's first words?

2 How good are people at characterizing the language of young children? This project is an extension of **Exercise 1.5** which allows you to apply the knowledge gained in **Units 1–10**. Ask a 5-year-old, a young teenager and an adult to have a brief conversation with you in which they pretend to be a 2-year-old. Tape-record the conversations. How closely do these conversations recreate the way toddlers pronounce their words and structure their sentences? Did you observe any differences between the child, the teenager and the adult in terms of their ability to recreate the language of young children? You could extend this project by comparing the performances of adults who come into prolonged daily contact with young children and those who do not, or by comparing two 5-year-olds, one who is the youngest or only child in the family and one with a younger brother or sister. As an alternative to using real people, you could apply a similar analysis to excerpts from children's literature which attempt to recreate the speech of young children.

3 When children overextend words in their spontaneous speech or fail to produce the name of an object, does this necessarily mean that they do not understand those words when they hear them? A 2-year-old child would be ideal for this mini-experiment, although you could extend the study to older or younger children or more than one 2-year-old.

Collect a series of colour photos of: three different domestic cats; three large felines (tiger, lion, leopard, etc.); three cat-size non-felines which nevertheless look similar to cats (guinea pig, rabbit, baby seal, etc.); three animals that look very unlike cats (elephant, crocodile, giraffe, etc.).

Shuffle the photos and show them to the child one at a time, asking 'What is this animal called?' Carefully note the response in each case including 'don't knows', hesitations, and self-corrections. Then lay out all twelve photos in front of the child and ask the child to 'Point to a picture of a cat', 'Point to a picture of a giraffe' and so on until you have used all ten animal names. Record all responses.

Did you find any differences between comprehension and production? For example, did the child answer 'Don't know' or answer incorrectly when asked to name an animal, but nevertheless point to the correct picture when asked? Did you find any response differences between the large felines and the cat-like non-felines? If you tried this on more than one child, were there any similarities or differences between the children? Work in this area was carried out by Thomson and Chapman (1977) who found that overextension in children's comprehension of words occurs much less frequently than in their production.

4 Investigate a child's understanding of spatial adjectives by playing 'The Opposite Game'. Here, 4- to 5-year-olds would be ideal, but you could extend this mini-experiment to 3- and 6-year-olds as well. This project is based on work carried out by Eve Clark (1972).

You will need two glove puppets for this game which will be named 'Ippo' and 'Oppo'. Show the child the puppets and say that Oppo always says just the opposite of what Ippo says. Demonstrate this with some easy pairs like *happy/sad*, *good/bad* etc. Then give Oppo to the child to operate while you keep Ippo. Begin with two or three easy pairs to make sure the child understands the game. Then ask the child the spatial adjectives given in **Table 3.1**, p. 17. Run through all the pairs once, giving the child the positive member of each pair. For example, Ippo says 'High' to which Oppo should say 'Low'. Carefully note the child's responses each time, including 'don't knows', hesitations and self-corrections. Then try running through the pairs again, this time using the negative member of each pair.

You can analyse your results in a variety of ways. Which adjective pairs proved easiest for the child? If you used more than one child, were their responses similar? Did the positive members of the pairs prove easier for the child? Were your results in broad agreement with the order of difficulty given in **Table 3.1**? Where the children gave inappropriate responses, how inappropriate were they? For example, did they get the positive/negative aspect right such as saying 'Little' where 'Short' was required? Did any responses include other appropriate meaning elements such as saying 'Down' where 'Low' was the expected answer?

5 Investigate how adults explain word meanings to children. Using a children's dictionary such as *The Oxford Illustrated Junior Dictionary*, *The Puffin Junior Dictionary* or *The Young Person's Picture Dictionary*, compare the definitions of three nouns, three verbs and three adjectives with the definitions given in an adult dictionary. Do you notice any differences in the ways word meanings are explained to young children? How would you characterize these differences? You could also compare the definitions given for the same words in two or more children's dictionaries.

You could extend this project by giving adults at least three of the words you used in the dictionary comparison and asking them to give you a definition of each word. Then ask them how they would explain the meaning of each of those words to a 3-year-old. Tape-record both sets of definitions. What differences (if any) did you notice between the two sets of definitions?

**UNITS
4 AND 5**

6 How closely do children's imitations of adult sentences match the structure of sentences they produce for themselves? Record a conversation with a 2½-year-old. You should find that the child's speech is still quite telegraphic. Then ask the child to **imitate** sentences like these:

> He kicked a red ball.
> Give the bottles to me.
> The cow likes the cat.
> A frog can jump very high.
> They were playing with me.

Analyse both the model sentences and the child's imitations in terms of the semantic roles expressed. Compare the child's imitations to your model sentences. What elements did the child omit? If any *content* words were omitted, which semantic roles did they express? If any *function* words were omitted, classify them as **articles**, **prepositions**, **verb *to be***, **auxiliary verbs**. Look also for the omission of word endings. Did the child change the word order at all? Did the imitations preserve the meaning of the originals? Then compare the child's **spontaneously produced sentences** to the imitations. Do they show similar structures and omissions?

You could extend this study by also asking the child to imitate some of the sentences that he or she had produced in the recorded conversation. Did the child's imitation match the spontaneously produced sentences when they were repeated out of context? Bloom and

Lightbown (1974) raised an intriguing point about children's imitations. They collected samples of a child's spontaneous sentences, some of which were quite long, even though the average length of the child's utterances at the time was about two words. The experimenter then spoke the same sentence the following day and asked the child to imitate it. The imitations were nowhere near as complex as the sentences which the child had spontaneously produced the day before. Here is one example:

> A: Can you say 'I'm trying to get this cow in here'?
> C: Cow in here.

7 Investigate a 5-year-old's understanding of sentences like *The wolf was bitten by the duck*; or *The monkey is being chased by the lion*. These are called PASSIVE SENTENCES. They occur more often in written language than in spoken language where it is more usual to say *The duck bit the wolf*; or *The lion is chasing the monkey*. In passive constructions the semantic **affected** is in grammatical subject position and the **agent** follows the preposition *by*. Even 5-year-old children can find these passive constructions very difficult to understand.

Passive sentence

You will need several small plastic animals. Explain that you want the child to help you act out a story with the animals. Try a practice run with a few simple sentences like *The horse sat on the cow*. The child should make the horse sit on the cow. Or *The horse kissed the cow*. The child should make the horse kiss the cow. Then try several sentences like these:

> The horse was kicked by the cow.
> The pig was knocked down by the horse.
> The cow was bitten by the lion.

Be sure to include some very unlikely events like *The lion was eaten by the duck* or *The elephant was knocked down by the pig*.

Did the child appear to understand any of these sentences? How consistent were the child's responses? Did the child have more trouble with the unlikely events? Did the child seem to be following a rule like first noun mentioned = agent; second noun = affected? Or did the child also use knowledge about the way the world usually works, assuming for example that a bigger animal will knock down a smaller one or that lions always do the eating and biting? Both Cromer (1991) and Roeper (1982) discuss children's understanding of passive sentences.

8 Collect a number of negative sentences from a 2- to 3-year-old child and see what rules the child is using at that stage in his or her development. Comparing two or more children would make this project even more interesting. One way of eliciting negative sentences is to say something that is obviously wrong. Children quite enjoy contradicting adults. Here are three examples, but remember

UNIT 6

they may not always work so it is a good idea to have plenty of 'extras'.

    a. Pick up a doll and say *What a big ball this is!*
    b. Say *I'm going to eat a chair for dinner.*
    c. There are no cars in the room (real or toy). Say *Can you please bring me the red car?*

You could further analyse your data by classifying the child's negatives according to meaning type as you did in **Exercise 6.9**. Bloom (1970) found that children tend to produce more adult forms when they are expressing 'non-existence' rather than when they are expressing 'denial'. Did you find a similar trend in your data?

9 Investigate a 2- to 3-year-old child's understanding of WH questions. You could try this with only one child, but it would be very interesting to have data from three or four children so that you can look for similarities and differences. Talk with the child while you are drawing pictures or playing with toy animals. Slip in a variety of WH questions and note down in each case whether the child gave an appropriate answer. Obviously your questions will have to be ones which naturally arise out of the situation, but here are some possible examples:

    Where is the horse?
    Why did you pick that crayon?
    What am I drawing?
    Who is sitting on the floor?
    When are we eating?

Ervin-Tripp (1970) found that young children understand and answer correctly *where*, *what* and *who* questions more easily than *how*, *why* and *when* questions. Did you find something similar?

UNIT 7

10 Do 5-year-olds have 'rules' for making plurals which they can use even with words they have never heard before? This project is similar to the pioneer 'wug' experiments carried by Jean Berko in 1958. You will need to make seven pairs of line drawings, one with cats and six with imaginary animals. Each pair will consist of a drawing of one animal and a drawing of two of those animals. Assign each of these names to an imaginary animal pair: *bleem*, *foo*, *niss*, *muzz*, *brop*, *dit*.

Start with the 'cat' pair. Show the child the drawing with one cat and say: 'This animal is called a "cat". What is this animal called?' (here the child should supply *cat*). 'In this picture there is one . . .' (here the child should again supply *cat*). Next, show the child the drawing of two cats and say: 'Now there are two . . .' (here the child should supply the plural form, *cats*).

With luck, the child will understand the game and then you can run through each of the imaginary animal pairs in the same way. It would be preferable to tape-record the responses, but you can write them down as long as you listen very carefully to the actual sounds of the plural endings. As adults we would expect the plurals of the imaginary words to sound like this: *bleemz, fooz, nissiz, muzziz, brops, dits*.

To what extent did the child's plurals meet your expectations? You could extend this mini-experiment to more than one 5-year-old or to younger children (although they may need more than one pair of practice pictures before they get the hang of it).

11 Try to get one or more young children (between 3 and 5 years old) to use some of the word-coining processes discussed in **Unit 7**, and analyse what types of word-coining processes they use. This project is similar to the experiments carried out by Clark and Hecht (1982). Here are some suggestions for the type of questions that you could ask:

> a. What do you call someone who catches things?
> b. What do you call someone who is covered in crumbs?
> c. What do you call something that crushes things?
> d. What do you call someone who plays music?
> e. What do you call something that blows bubbles?

You will probably need to ask about twenty such questions if you hope to get some examples of spontaneous word inventions. For example, be prepared for children to give answers like 'Silly' to question **b**. The answer is very apt, but not much help when you are looking for things like 'Crumby' or 'Crumb-man.'

UNIT 8

12 Do even young children change their conversational style depending on who their partner is? Observe a 4- to 5-year-old child in conversation with another child of his or her own age and with an adult. If at all possible, tape-record the conversations, but also take notes about the surrounding context of the conversation. Discuss any differences you observed between the two conversations in terms of:

> a. the child's tone of voice;
> b. conversation topics;
> c. the degree of politeness;
> d. the length of the child's sentences;
> e. the number of questions and commands;
> f. any other differences you may have noted.

You could extend this project by observing children in conversations where their partners are much younger than they are or by observing them playing with two types of dolls, one which is clearly a baby and the other which is more 'grown up' like *Barbie* or *Action Man*. What differences did you notice when the child was talking to a real (or imaginary) younger child? Work on this aspect of children's conversational development has been carried out by (among others) Sachs and Devin (1976).

13 How do parents change their conversational style when speaking to their young children? Are there any aspects to their 'child-style' which might aid language development? This area of research was pioneered by Snow (1977). Observe a parent in conversation with his or her child (preferably a 2- to 3-year-old) and with another adult. Discuss any differences you noted in the parent's conversational style in the two situations in terms of:

a. tone of voice, speed of speech, number of pauses;
b. length and complexity of sentences;
c. number of questions and commands;
d. number of repetitions or rephrasings of what either the parent or their conversational partner said;
e. conversational topics;
f. any other differences you might have noticed.

14 To what extent do children alter their conversation depending on what they think their listener already knows? This project is based on work done by Maratsos (1973). You will need a 4- to 5-year-old child and an adult helper for this project. Find a colour picture with some sort of activity going on involving two or more people or animals (picture story-books for the under-fives can be a good source). While both you and the child are looking at the picture, ask the child to tell you what is going on in the picture.

Then, bring your helper into the room. Put a blindfold on your helper and ask the child to tell your friend what is going on in the picture. What differences, if any, did you notice in the two descriptions? Look particularly at the use of *the/a* and pronouns, as well as at the detail of the description and the order in which various aspects of the picture are discussed. If you tried this with more than one child, what similarities and differences did you notice between the children?

**UNITS
9 AND 10**

15 While English has several standard 'baby-talk' words, individual families often have their own additional set. Ask at least four families with young children for a list of *all* the baby-talk words the family uses and their meanings. Words relating to food and drink, family members, animals, and potty training are the ones most likely to be expressed in this way. Transcribe both the baby-talk words and their 'translations'. Then analyse these lists in further detail in terms of:

a. the phonological simplifications present in each of the baby-talk words;
b. any similarities or differences between families in terms of the types of simplification processes used;
c. any similarities or differences between the families in terms of the items that tend to be expressed with baby-talk;
d. how many of these words were initiated by the parents, for example, using *wee-wee* for *urinate*, and how many were adult reactions to the children's own pronunciations.

16 Make a profile of a child's current phonological development. Show the child some familiar objects (about ten) and ask the child to name them. Carefully note down and transcribe the target word and the child's actual pronunciation. Choose objects whose names involve the various potential 'problem' areas of pronunciation that we have discussed in these units such as words containing **consonant clusters**, **word-final consonants**, **syllabic *l* or *n***, or **more than one syllable**. Your words should include a variety of consonant types: **voiced**, **voiceless**, **stops**, **fricatives** and **nasals**. Check your list of targets with the child's parents to make sure these words are already in use by the child. A child of 2½ usually has a sufficiently large spoken vocabulary for a study like this.

In addition, you can also ask the child to **imitate** a variety of unusual words not currently in his or her vocabulary such as *zinc* or *mandarin*. You can present this as a game where the child repeats everything you say. It is a good idea to begin with a few words that the child already uses to make sure he or she understands the game and then move on to the more unusual words. Again keep a careful record of the target word and the child's actual pronunciation.

Your profile should note both the instances where the child uses the adult pronunciation and those where the child's pronunciation deviates from the adult target. What types of sounds or combinations of sounds tend to pose difficulties? What processes are at work where the child appears to deviate from the adult pronunciation? Are there any observable patterns? Do you notice any differences between situations where the child is spontaneously producing a familiar word and situations where the child is imitating a 'new' word? If you have time, you could visit the child two or three months later and repeat your investigation, noting any changes that have occurred.

17 Are children aware of their own pronunciations? This aspect of children's phonological development was investigated by (among others) Smith (1973). Find at least four or five words which a child consistently 'mispronounces' using the techniques discussed in the previous project. Parents may be able to point you in the right direction here, having already observed several such words. After getting the child to produce these words spontaneously, ask the child to imitate your (adult) pronunciations. Carefully note any hestitations or self-corrections which the child makes. Were there any differences between the child's spontaneous productions and the imitations? Finally, ask the child to show you the objects in question using the child's own pronunciation. Did the child appear to understand you when you used this pronunciation? Did the child show any signs of hestitation or surprise upon hearing you use his pronunciation or make any comments on your pronunciation? Some children say things like 'You didn't say "wabbit" wight' or 'That's not a "fiss" (fish), it's a FISS!'

18 What can children's spelling errors reveal about their underlying knowledge of the sounds of spoken language? Learning how to write is not easy. As we saw in **Unit 9**, the written form of English gives only an approximation of what a word actually sounds like. The alphabet contains twenty-six letters which must be used to represent well over forty distinct English speech sounds. English spelling also has considerable irregularities. For example note the very different spoken forms of *-ough* in *bough* and *cough*. Gentry and Gillett (1993) have proposed that children in the early stages of learning how to write go through a stage where their spelling is phonetically based, somewhat like the phonetic spelling we used in **Exercise 9.2.** While children's early attempts at spelling can seem quaint, to say the least, their mistakes can be quite revealing of their considerable knowledge of how their language actually sounds. We can see this in the following passage written by a 7-year-old British child:

> Jesus ast his mother wey is evrey one so sad? because there is no wine left ansed Mary ... The cooks were cros but they obade.

The use of *ast* for *asked* (spoken form: **askt**) suggests that this child, in common with many young children (and adults in rapid speech), deletes the **k** from the three consonant cluster **skt**. The omission of 'silent' letters is also very common. Note how the 'h' in *why* and the 'w' and 'r' in *answered* do not appear in the child's versions. The child's spelling of *cross* reflects the fact that, although many words in English are written with a 'double consonant', the consonant is only pronounced once, not twice, in the spoken form.

Obtain several examples of stories written by 5–7-year-olds. (A visit to your local school should provide you with plenty of examples.) Analyse the instances where the children appear to be using a fairly accurate phonetic form of spelling even though it is not the conventional spelling of written English. If you manage to obtain early and later writing samples from the same child, look for instances where the phonetic spelling is in transition to a more conventional form. For example, the child's spelling of *obeyed* in the passage above accurately conveys the sound similarity with words like *made* and *spade* and uses the written convention of the silent 'e'.

GOING ON FROM HERE: CENTRAL ISSUES AND STUDY QUESTIONS

12

> This is the final unit, but of course it is only the beginning of the story. In this unit we look at some issues which are central to language acquisition research and suggest other aspects of language development which we have not been able to cover in this workbook but which are nevertheless fascinating areas of study.

CENTRAL ISSUES

Now that you have completed this workbook, you have a fairly good idea of the complexity and abstract nature of human language with all its various systems of sound, grammar and meaning. How can we explain children's ability to acquire so much knowledge about these systems in such a short space of time? The question is a very old one but it is still central to language acquisition research today.

If you look in books about children's language written before the late 1950s, you will find that language acquisition is often referred to as the 'acquisition of verbal habits'. This reflects the ideas of behaviourist psychologists like B.F. Skinner and his predecessors who viewed children's language learning as a rather passive process of imitating the speech they heard from adults, accompanied by positive reinforcement when they got it 'right' and negative reinforcement when they got it 'wrong'. In other words, there was no essential difference between the way a rat learns to negotiate a maze and a child learns to speak. The problem with the notion of reinforcement is that it is hard to see quite how it would work with young children. As you have seen in the conversations in the **Corpus**, parents put a lot of effort into keeping children's conversations going, but only very rarely do they explicitly approve or disapprove of their children's grammar. When they do comment in some way about mistakes, we often see that the children either 'miss the point' or resolutely stick to their version. There are even bigger problems with imitation. Children do sometimes imitate what they hear, but they clearly do much more than that. They also use rules to produce forms of the language that they could not have heard from adults – words like *mouses* and *hitted*, for example.

These kinds of counter-arguments were used by the American linguist Noam Chomsky (1959) in his criticism of the behaviourist approach to language acquisition. In contrast to Skinner (1957), Chomsky proposed that children actively construct the rule systems of their native language aided by a brain already 'set up' with a special language capacity that is separate from other types of mental abilities. Chomsky's ideas have been and continue to be enormously influential. Since the late 1950s there has been an explosion of research into children's language, some of which has been aimed at finding evidence to support Chomsky's ideas. Other research has been aimed at finding counter-evidence for his ideas or evidence for differing approaches. For example, much of the research into child-directed language and the early social interaction between mothers and babies was a response, at least in part, to Chomsky's view that the 'poverty of the input' makes it impossible for children to acquire a system as abstract and complex as human language without some inborn knowledge about the way it works. That is, knowledge about the general principles that all the world's languages obey, and knowledge about the 'permitted' ways that languages can vary from one another.

The ideas of the Swiss psychologist Jean Piaget (1959) have been another major influence on the study of language development. Although he died in 1980, Piaget's proposals continue to stimulate a great deal of interesting research on the relationship between language and thought in children. Like Chomsky, Piaget viewed the child as actively constructing language rather than simply imitating it. Unlike Chomsky, however, Piaget did not view the human mind as having a separate language processing capacity or any inborn knowledge about language. For Piaget, the only language learning equipment that a child is born with is a strong instinct to reach out to and make sense of the world and a brain uniquely adapted to extracting patterns and solving puzzles. In this view, language is just one of the many 'puzzles' that children solve as they grow up and should be studied in the context of the child's overall intellectual and social development. One aspect of Piaget's original thinking on language acquisition that has proved controversial is the idea that language acquisition is dependent on or 'driven' by children's cognitive development (the development of their thinking and reasoning powers and their understanding of the world). In other words, children need to understand a concept before they can map it on to language. One problem with this idea is that, in theory, children with severe mental handicaps should not be able to acquire fluent language. However, as Richard Cromer (1991) has pointed out, many of these children do just that. Recent research also indicates that sometimes language development may actually precede and stimulate some kinds of cognitive development.

The exciting thing about the study of language acquisition is that there is still no one theory or approach which has all the answers. Nevertheless, a great deal of progress has been made in the last forty years. We know much more about what children do as they acquire language, and not simply English speaking children – the data set is much richer now. We have increasingly sophisticated ways of testing the linguistic and non-linguistic knowledge available to even tiny infants. And finally, we have arrived at some potentially more fruit-ful ways of thinking about the 'problem':

- Language is seen not only as a form of behaviour to be acquired but also as a structural system to be acquired, where vocabulary, grammar, and conversational skills may each involve quite differ-ent acquisition mechanisms.
- Children are no longer seen as passive learners being 'taught' their native language but rather as central and active participants in the acquisition process.
- The focus has shifted away from debating 'nature versus nurture' to examining the ways in which nature and nurture interact in the successful acquisition of language.
- Research now looks not only at changes in the quantity of chil-dren's knowledge about their native language but also at changes in the quality of that knowledge. Language development can be viewed as a process that involves children restructuring their knowledge into new mental representations of language which are increasingly more flexible, sophisticated and abstract.

1 We began this workbook by analysing children's first words. But clearly, a great deal of pre-linguistic development had to happen before those first words could emerge. What preparations for lan-guage have taken place between the time a newborn baby cries from hunger and the 1-year-old toddler says 'bottle!'?

2 Many of the world's children learn and use more than one lan-guage. Some start in infancy, others only after they have begun school or moved to another country. How can a multilingual environment affect the course of language acquisition? What can we learn from the language development of bilingual children?

3 Learning to read and write builds upon the earlier acquisition of spoken language and leads to yet further linguistic development. How do children's language skills grow and change during the school years?

4 Some children acquire language in exceptional circumstances. Language acquisition research has helped speech therapists and psy-chologists to understand the difficulties that children in exceptional circumstances can sometimes face. In turn, studies of atypical language development have provided valuable insights into the mechanisms

STUDY QUESTIONS

involved in ordinary language acquisition. What is the course of language development like for children with visual or hearing impairments, learning disabilities, or autism?

Metalinguistic awareness

5 Five-year-old children can comment on their own and other people's language, play with words and speech sounds just as they do with their toys, and enjoy all sorts of jokes and riddles based on the unusual or unexpected use of language. In other words, children not only learn to speak a language, they also learn to think and talk about language itself. This ability is called METALINGUISTIC AWARENESS. How does this ability grow and develop in childhood?

FURTHER READING

These books assume little or no prior knowledge of linguistics and are specifically aimed at readers who are just starting their study of children's language development.

Aitchison, J. (1994) *Words in the Mind*, Oxford: Blackwell. Aitchison provides a fascinating introduction to word meaning and to the way the human mind stores and processes words. The book has chapters dealing specifically with children's acquisition of word meanings and the sound structure of words.

Aitchison, J. (1998) (4th edn) *The Articulate Mammal*, London: Routledge. This is a lively introduction to psycholinguistics, the study of how we acquire, produce and understand language, with several chapters devoted to language acquisition.

Crystal, D. (1986) *Listen to Your Child*, Harmondsworth: Penguin. This is an easy to read and non-technical account of children's language development year by year.

Donaldson, M. (1987) *Children's Minds*, London: Fontana. An excellent basic introduction to the development of thought and language in both early childhood and the school years. Donaldson is especially good at describing and clarifying Piaget's approach to children's intellectual development.

Grosjean, F. (1987) *Life with Two Languages: An Introduction to Bilingualism*, Cambridge, MA: Harvard. Written in an accessible style, this book has an interesting and wide-ranging chapter on the bilingual child.

Pinker, S. (1994) *The Language Instinct*, Harmondsworth: Penguin. A thought-provoking book about human language for the general reader. Chapters 9 and 10 deal specifically with language acquisition and provide accessible and often witty explanations of Chomsky's theories.

BEGINNER LEVEL

As you have seen, the analysis of sentence structure and speech sounds is particularly important for studying children's language development. The following books, while assuming no prior knowledge of linguistics, will help you to further develop your analytic skills in these areas.

Ashby, P. (1995) *Speech Sounds*, London: Routledge. This workbook gives you hands-on experience of describing and classifying speech sounds in much greater detail than has been possible in **Units 9 and 10** and teaches you how to transcribe speech using the International Phonetic Alphabet.

Thomas, L. (1993) *Beginning Syntax*, Oxford: Blackwell. A very clear and helpful introduction to the analysis of English sentence structures. It has graded exercises with answers so that you can check your understanding as you go along.

**INTER-
MEDIATE
LEVEL**

Bishop, D. and Mogford, K. (eds) (1993) *Language Development in Exceptional Circumstances*, Hove: Lawrence Erlbaum. A series of articles written in a very accessible style about children acquiring language in a wide range of 'exceptional' circumstances including twinship, bilingualism, extreme deprivation, visual or hearing impairments, learning disabilities and autism. The final article deals with how studies of language acquisition in these circumstances can shed light on the mechanisms involved in 'normal' development. The book has a very helpful glossary.

Bishop, D. (1997) *Uncommon Understanding*, Hove: Psychology Press. Most books on language acquisition tend to concentrate on language production rather than comprehension. This clearly written and well-illustrated book redresses the balance and includes some fascinating data. While its emphasis is on children with an impaired ability to understand language, normal development in this area is also given extensive coverage.

Foster, S. (1990) *The Communicative Competence of Young Children*, Harlow: Longman. This briefly covers the necessary background concepts in linguistics before moving on to discuss recent research into all aspects of normal language development in children up to the age of five, including the social and conversational aspects. Foster is particularly good at succinctly explaining and evaluating different theories of language acquisition.

Gleason, J. (ed.) (1997) *The Development of Language*, Boston: Allyn and Bacon. Highly recommended. Each chapter is written by an expert in the field. The book is well illustrated and covers all aspects of language development including communication skills in babies, learning how to have socially appropriate conversations, development in exceptional circumstances, and language and literacy in the school years.

Bloom, P. (ed.) (1993) *Language Acquisition: Core Readings*, Cambridge, MA: MIT Press. The editor describes this book as a snapshot of the theory and research taking place in language acquisition in the 1990s. The eighteen articles, some of which are quite challenging, concentrate on the theoretical debates in the areas of vocabulary and grammar development. I suggest you start with the 'Overview' article by Paul Bloom and the short but fascinating article by Richard Cromer, 'Language growth with experience without feedback'.

Clark, E. (1993) *The Lexicon in Acquisition*, Cambridge: Cambridge University Press. Although this is an advanced level book, it is well worth the effort, especially for those with a special interest in children's vocabulary development. Clark gives clear explanations of the basic concepts used in lexical semantics (the study of word meaning) and provides a wealth of fascinating child data from English and several other languages.

Ingram, D. (1989) *First Language Acquisition*, Cambridge: Cambridge University Press. This book is not an easy read, but its strong point lies in the descriptions of many key studies in language development. In addition to reporting the results of the studies and their implications, Ingram also describes in some detail the actual methods the researchers used.

The following are the sources for the research mentioned in the units and for the individual examples of children's language which have been used in and sometimes adapted for this workbook. Some of these books and articles are quite advanced but the work of most of the authors is also summarized and explained in the books suggested above.

Bellugi, U. (1967) 'The acquisition of negation', unpublished doctoral dissertation, Harvard University.

—— (1971) 'Simplification in children's language' in R. Huxley and E. Ingram (eds), *Language Acquisition: Models and Methods*, NY: Academic Press.

Berko, J. (1958) 'The child's learning of English morphology', *Word*, 14: 150–77.

Bloom, L. (1970) *Language Development: Form and Function in Emerging Grammars*, Cambridge, MA: MIT Press.

Bloom, L. and Lahey, M. (1978) *Language Development and Language Disorders*, NY: John Wiley and Sons.

Bloom, L. and Lightbown, P. (1974) 'Imitation in language development', *Cognitive Psychology*, 6: 380–420.

Bowerman, M. (1982a) 'Reorganizational processes in lexical and syntactic development' in E. Wanner and L. Gleitman (eds) *Language Acquisition: The State of the Art*, Cambridge: Cambridge University Press.

—— (1982b) 'Hidden meaning: The role of covert conceptual structures in children's development of language' in D. Rogers and J. Sloboda (eds) *The Acquisition of Symbolic Skills*, NY: Plenum.

Brown, R. (1976) *A First Language*, Harmondsworth: Penguin.

Casagrande, J. (1964) 'Comanche baby language' in D. Hymes (ed.) *Language in Culture and Society*, NY: Harper and Row.

Chomsky, N. (1959) 'A review of B.F. Skinner's *Verbal Behavior*', *Language*, 35: 26–58.

Clark, E. (1972) 'On the child's acquisition of antonyms in two semantic fields', *Journal of Verbal Learning and Verbal Behavior*, 11: 750–8.

—— (1973) 'What's in a word? On the child's acquisition of semantics in his first language' in T. Moore (ed.) *Cognitive Development and the Acquisition of Language*, NY: Academic Press.

—— (1982) 'The young wordmaker: A case study of innovation in the child's lexicon' in E. Wanner and L. Gleitman (eds) *Language Acquisition: The State of the Art*, Cambridge: Cambridge University Press.

Clark, E. and Hecht, B. (1982) 'Learning to coin agent and instrument nouns', *Cognition* 12: 1–24.

Cromer, R. (1991) *Language and Thought in Normal and Handicapped Children*, Oxford: Blackwell.

Dale, P. (1976) *Language Development*, NY: Holt, Rinehart and Wilson.

de Villiers, J. and de Villiers, P. (1978) *Language Acquisition*, Cambridge, MA: Harvard University Press.

Ervin-Tripp, S. (1970) 'Discourse agreement: How children answer questions' in J. Hayes (ed.) *Cognition and the Development of Language*, NY: John Wiley and Sons.

Fletcher, P. (1988) *A Child's Learning of English*, Oxford: Blackwell.

Gentry, J. and Gillett, J. (1993) *Teaching Kids to Spell*, Portsmouth, NH: Heinemann.

Ingram, D. (1986) 'Phonological development: production' in P. Fletcher and M. Garman (eds) *Language Acquisition*, 2nd edn, Cambridge: Cambridge University Press.

Maratsos, M. (1973) 'Non-egocentric communications in pre-school children', *Child Development*, 44: 607–700.

Nelson, K. (1973) 'Structure and strategy in learning to talk', *Monograph of the Society for Research in Child Development*, 38, no. 149.

Piaget, J. (1959) *The Language and Thought of the Child*, 3rd edn, London: Routledge.

Rescorla, L. (1980) 'Overextensions in early language development', *Journal of Child Language*, 7: 321–35.

Roeper, T. (1982) 'The role of universals in the acquisition of gerunds' in E. Wanner and L. Gleitman (eds) *Language Acquisition: The State of the Art*, Cambridge: Cambridge University Press.

Sachs, J. and Devin, J. (1976) 'Young children's use of age appropriate speech styles in social interaction and role playing', *Journal of Child Language*, 3: 81–98.

Shatz, M. (1982) 'On mechanisms of language acquisition: Can features of the communicative environment account for development?' in E. Wanner and L. Gleitman (eds) *Language Acquisition: The State of the Art*, Cambridge: Cambridge University Press.

Skinner, B. (1957) *Verbal Behavior*, NY: Appleton-Century-Crofts.

Smith, N. (1973) *The Acquisition of Phonology*, Cambridge: Cambridge University Press.

Snow, C. (1977) 'Mother's speech research: from input to interaction' in C. Snow and C. Ferguson (eds) *Talking to Children: Language Input and Acquisition*, Cambridge: Cambridge University Press.

Thomson, J. and Chapman, R. (1977) 'Who is "Daddy" revisited: the status of two year olds' overextended words in use and comprehension', *Journal of Child Language*, 4: 359–75.

Weir, R. (1962) *Language in the Crib*, The Hague: Mouton.

CORPUS OF CHILD-LANGUAGE DATA

This corpus consists of speech and dialogue samples from a variety of children. **Corpora I** and **II** will give indications where the child's pronunciation has substantially deviated from the adult targets for use with **Units 9** and **10**. (Children's pronunciations are printed in **bold** letters.) However, for ease of reading, the remaining sections are transcribed into the 'adult' form. The ages of the children (where indicated) are given in years and months. In the dialogues, 'C' = child; 'M' = mother; 'A' = other adult. Hesitations in speech are indicated by — . Information to help you interpret the conversations is contained in brackets.

CORPUS I: SAMPLE OF CHILDREN'S EARLY WORD COMBINATIONS

1. take **manana** (banana)
2. me not **tit** (sit)
3. mummy **gib** (give)
4. mummy **gup** (cup)
5. baby **krip** (crib)
6. me **lili** (little)
7. no see **guk** (duck)
8. this not **bu** (blue)
9. **gu** here (glue)
10. it not **lu** off (flew)
11. can't see **lap** (flap)
12. no me **leep** (sleep)
13. **kok** ticking (clock)
14. **lug** icky (slug)
15. daddy **kik** (stick)
16. big **mipu** (nipple)
17. me got **apmə** (asthma)
18. no more **handu** (handle)
19. bus **litu** no (little)
20. it **bitu** me (bitten)
21. eat **ola** (granola = cereal)
22. no **fat** (flat)
23. give me **ratu** (rattle)
24. allgone **ti** (twig)
25. more **bəred** (bread)
26. **melə** yucky (smell)

**CORPUS II:
SOPHIE**

Dialogues 1–10. Age 2;4

1. C: me want that.
    M: what is it?
    C: **seen**.
    M: plasticine?
    C: mmm.

2. C: you take a **bissy**.
    M: 'cause I was hungry.
    C: me want a **bissy**.
    C: (later) you put **bissy** on there.
    M: I didn't put biscuit on there.
    C: (later) me want **nother bissy**.

3. C: Daddy come down too.
    M: who's coming down too?
    C: Daddy.
    M: Daddy? no. where's Daddy?
    C: me want—Daddy come down.
    M: working sweetie.
    C: (referring to Daddy) no. no. find her cheque-book.
    M: finding her cheque-book.

4. C: me want that **pano**.
    M: you've got a real piano.
    C: why?
    M: it's upstairs.
    C: why? why?
    M: what do you mean why?
    C: why?

5. C: me want to read that.
    M: okay. let's read that.
    C: read that. wrong side.
    M: I think you've got it upside down.
    C: look. look her toe.
    M: I think they're funny shoes actually. made to look like toes.
    C: Why?

6. C: our play that. on floor. our play that on floor. now.
    M: alright—
    C: Mummy. come on floor me.

7. C: that one broke
    M: oh. when did that happen?
    C: Muffy step on that.
    M: who stepped on that?
    C: Muffy. (a friend)
    M: Muffy stepped on it.

8. C: me—me want make house you.
   M: yes —
   C: me want house for Kate. me want make house for Kate. you—you help. you make house for Kate.

9. C: children in there. where's the childrens?
   M: the children? there they are.
   C: all those children. me playing all those children.

10. C: her—her got **blanky**. her want a **blanky**. where's **blanky**?
    M: I don't think we've got a blanket.

Dialogues 11–15. Age 3;0

11. (M. picks up counter and slips it through the side of 'Snakes and Ladders' box)
    C: why did you post it through, Mummy?
    M: post it?
    C: put it there—

12. C: me did some of those, Mummy.
    M: did you?
    C: when you been tidying up. just been leaved there, Mummy.

13. C: shall me sit **mon** (on) my legs? **mon** my bottom?
    M: mmhm.
    C: why did— why did— Mummy why— why did—Hester be fast asleep.
    M: she was tired.
    C: and why did her have two sweets?

14. (still talking about Hester)
    C: why did you give her—to her when her been flu?
    M: to cheer her up.
    C: what did her have wrong with her?
    M: flu.
    C: why—why do—me—why didn't me get flu ever?
    M: I don't know. you didn't get it. did you. that time.
    C: why didn't me get flu?
    M: because you're so healthy.
    C: why are me so health—healthy?
    M: you're such a fatty.

15. (sees two painted plates, one large and one small)
    C: what—what are these pictures doing here?
    M: careful of them darling. Gangan (grandmother) painted them.
    C: me like a little one best.
    M: do you—?
    C: which one do you like first? a big one or a little one?
    M: I like that white one.

Dialogues 16–21. Age 3;5

16. M: which songs did you—did you do?
    C: I **gotten**.
    M: oh Sophie. you can't have forgotten already.
    C: I have. was so long. I **gotten**.

17. (playing the recorder)
    C: shall I do that one? I play it with my **corder**. it supposed
       to go on **corder**.
    C: (later) what did you hear of that?
    M: I think I liked the first one better.
    C: (plays again) what did you hear of that?
    M: that was very nice.
    C: (plays again) what did you think of that?
    M: I thought that was very nice.

18. M: Daddy said he could hear you. at Matthew's. d'you
       know that?
    C: it wasn't me.
    M: wasn't it?
    C: it was Matthew shouting.
    M: was he being naughty?
    C: mmm. and he was crying.

19. (M. has just explained why C. can't use the phone)
    C: why? I want to ring up somebody. and her won't be
       there tomorrow. her won't be there.
    M: who won't?
    C: um—and me have got to ring up. her won't be there.
    M: have to just try tomorrow and hope for the best.
    C: her—her will be there. her won't be there. her—I'll have
       to do it on—on Sunday.

20. C: why d'you never buy me a guitar?
    M: well I don't know. would you like one?
    C: yes.
    M: a little guitar.
    C: no a big one. a big one.
    M: you wouldn't be able to play a big one.
    C: I would. I would. I would be able to. I—I don't mind.
       (later) you's idiotic. where's my piano book gone to?
    M: I'm not idiotic.
    C: you are. you won't let me play a guitar. (now changing
       height of music stand) look. look.
    M: you're cheeky.
    C: I made it go smaller . . . can make it go—much higher.
    M: you won't be able to see it if it goes any higher.
    C: (later) can you make it go upper?
    M: more still?

21. C: shall we go down to Barnett's? (sweet shop)
    M: no. because we're waiting for Hester to come back.
    C: (later) while Hester's at school. we can buy—I can buy some sweets.
    M: she'll be back any minute lovey.
    C: oh. when her's at school.—I—I'll buy some sweeties.

Dialogues 22–6. Age 3;11

22. (looking at a picture book)
    M: that's an animal called an iguana. don't you like that?
    C: cover he's face.
    M: oh why? don't you like it?
    C: no he's—
    M: he's rather a friendly iguana.
    C: what are **guanas**?
    M: guanas. it's a sort of lizard—animal—green animal.

23. M: oh gosh, this is a long story.
    C: how d'you know?
    M: about Zozo. Zozo the monkey.
    C: can you read it to me?
    M: I'll read some of it.

24. C: I got a headache.
    M: oh darling. have you?
    C: mmm. can we have some cucumber for lunch?
    M: cucumber? yeah. if you want to.
    C: **cuz** I need some. I need a cool bit.
    M: you need some cucumber do you?
    C: **cuz** I need the cold bit to spread on my face and it goes away.
    M: oh Sophie.
    C: **cuz** it does, Mummy.
    M: yes. but who on earth have you seen putting cucumber on their face?
    C: what?
    M: who have you seen put cucumber on their face?
    C: Griselda.

25. (telling M. about a TV programme)
    C: um—um—he—he had his own room. and—he—he had a pointy thing. and a machine. you see.
    M: a machine.
    C: and—and—he heard he say. if you push that button again. and the man did. and you see. and—um—he—and he—and all the paper flied out inside.
    M: oh. because it was a wind machine.
    C: yes.

26. C: when is Daddy going to come back?
    M: quite soon. I think love.

C: at eight o'clock?
M: no. I hope he'll be back at one o'clock.
C: Mummy, he's going to be back at eight o'clock.
M: is he?

Reprinted with the permission of Macmillan Publishing Company from *Language Development and Language Disorders* by Lois Bloom and Margaret Lahey. Copyright 1978 by John Wiley and Sons.

CORPUS III: ALISON

1. Age 1;4
    C: (picks up toy cow) cow. cow. cow.
    C: (tries to stand it on chair) chair. chair.
    M: (C. gives cow to M. for help) what, darling?
    C: Mama.

2. Age 1;4
    C: (offers biscuit to M.) Mommy.
    M: oh, thank you.
    C: (looks at cups) juice.
    M: shall we have some juice?
    C: (looks in cup) cup. (picks up two cups and holds one cup out to M.) Mommy. juice.
    M: Mommy juice.
    C: No. (puts down one cup) Baby!
    M: Baby.
    C: (picks up other cup) Mommy. juice.

3. Age 1;9
    C: (wearing a jacket and pointing to her neck) up. up.
    M: what?
    C: neck. up.
    M: neck? what do you want? what?
    C: neck.
    M: what's on your neck?
    C: (points to zipper and lifts her chin up) zip. zip. zip.

4. Age 2;4
    C: (M. is wearing microphone) I want try that—that necklace.
    M: you want to try this necklace? okay. you know what this is called?
    C: something.
    M: see, it's a microphone. there. (puts microphone on Alison)
    C: I don't want it.
    M: you don't want it?
    C: no. you want it on. you have it on.

5. Age 2;4
    C: (climbing on chair) I'm gonna sit on here. may I? I wanna sit on here.

C: (later) oh I don't want drink it out cup. I want drink it out can.

M: oh, what did I say about that? what did I say about drinking it out of the can?

C: Mommy, I want it.

M: you want it?

C: I want drink it out can.

6. Age 2;10

M: (a baby boy is in the room) maybe he'd like to see the truck.

C: he—he may want to play with the truck.

M: okay.

C: maybe he'll play with the truck. he can play with the truck. I think he'll play with the truck.

M: yes. I think he likes the truck.

CORPUS IV: KATHRYN

Reprinted with the permission of Macmillan Publishing Company from *Language Development and Language Disorders* by Lois Bloom and Margaret Lahey. Copyright 1978 by John Wiley and Sons.

1. Age 1;9

C: (picks up red bean bag in shape of a frog) Santa Claus.

M: Santa Claus? that's a frog, honey. that's not Santa Claus. that's a frog. red frog.

C: frog. (puts frog on car) sits.

M: yes, he's sitting down. that's right.

2. Age 2;9

A: (language researcher has come to visit. C. hasn't seen her for six weeks) hi.

C: hi.

A: hi Kathryn. I haven't seen you in such long time.

C: you came. you come a lot of days.

A: I do come a lot.

C: you come lots of weeks. again and again and again.

A: I didn't come last week.

C: so you came this week.

3. Age 2;9

C: (looking under her skirt) I just have see. I'm gonna get some rubber pants.

A: why?

C: because then I won't go tinkle in these pants so I'll get some rubber pants.

A: why? do you think you'll need them?

C: yes.

A: you'll know if you wanta go tinkling.

C: but if I go tinkle in my pants—I have to get some of those rubber pants. (going into her bedroom) I'll be right back. the door is open so I can get in.

4. Age 2;11
    C: (playing 'airplane trip' with the language researcher) now, why don't we shut the doors?
    A: hmmm?
    C: why don't you shut your—shut your door? shut so no air can come in.
    A: I did.
    C: let's get. ssh! ssh! and some nurses bring some—some food.
    A: who?
    C: the—the—the—the—lady who lives in the airplane.
    A: who is the lady who lives in the airplane? what did you call her?
    C: a lady.
    A: did you call her a nurse or a stewardess?
    C: a stewardess.

CORPUS V: SPEECH FROM 3- TO 4-YEAR-OLDS

1. A: He's not coming home today. But he's coming soon, Jamie.
    C: Coming yesterday?

2. C: (trying to open a clip) How did you unsqueezed it?

3. C: (tidying up) I putted my room all clean.

4. C: (has been 'typing') I beed a good typewriter.

5. C: (crumpling a paper) There, I unflatted it.

6. C: (collapsing a telescope) I tooked it smaller.

7. C: I hate you and I'll never unhate you or nothing!
    M: What?
    C: I'll never like you.

8. C: (has nailed two pieces of wood together) I hammed those all by myself.

9. C: Nobody don't like me.
    M: No. Say 'nobody likes me'.
    C: Nobody don't like me. (above dialogue repeated 8 times)
    M: Now listen carefully. Say 'nobody LIKES me'.
    C: Oh . . . Nobody don't LIKES me.

10. C: Put me that broom. Let's get brooming.

11. A: What do you call someone who burns things?
    C: A fireman.

12. C: (Trying on a new jacket. Kojak is a TV detective noted for his tight-fitting clothes) It's too tight. I feel all Kojaky.

13. C: (wants M. to change sister's nappy before feeding her) Don't eat her yet. She's smelly!

14. C: (at breakfast) Why you didn't jam my bread?

15. C: He hitted me! He's a puncher he is. He's being badder
    and BADDER.

16. C: (has just sneezed 3 times) These flowers are sneezing
    me!

CORPUS VI:
HANNAH

Data collected by Gayle Croker.

Dialogues 1–9. Age 1;6. Hannah and her babysitter, Gayle, are in
Gayle's living room.

1. A: what can you hear? where's your mum, Hannah?
    C: gone uh walk.
    A: gone for a walk?
    C: (Hannah sees the tape recorder and its buttons) **pess.**
        pess. pess. ('press')
    A: don't press.
    C: **pess.**
    A: no.
    C: **pess.**
    A: no.
    C: **pess. nat** ('that') one. **dere** ('there'). **nat** one.

2. C: (wants to see her father) see dad.
    A: see dad?
    C: yeah.
    A: he's at home.
    C: yeah.
    A: your dad's at home.
    C: (pointing to ceiling) he up where.
    A: where's your mum?
    C: gone uh work.

3. C: it not heavy. (picking up a cushion)
    A: it's not heavy.
    C: yeah.
    A: oh.
    C: heavy. it heavy. (placing cushion on chair)
    C: (later the cushion falls off) come off. **dat** ('that') one go
        sit **nere** ('there'). it go sit **nere**.

4. A: are you tired?
    C: I tired.
    A: ah. go to sleep then baby. (tickles Hannah's feet)
    C: **top** ('stop') it. **top** it.
    A: why? why?
    C: no like it.

5. A: where's your drink?
    C: **dere**. ('there', pointing to tape-recorder)
    A: that's not your drink. what's that? tape-recorder.
    C: **teep corder**.
    A: tape-recorder.

6. (looking out the window, Hannah sees an elderly lady and birds
    in the front garden)
    C: **dere** Nana. (Hannah's name for her grandmother) birdie.
    A: the birdie?
    C: yeah.
    A: where?
    C: baby. (picking up a doll)

7. A: what ya havin' for your dinner?
    C: chicken.
    A: chicken?
    C: yeah.
    A: and what else?
    C: pot—potat—
    A: potatoes?
    C: potatoes.

8. C: come on.
    A: where?
    C: **uptairs** ('upstairs')
    A: where's Jayne and Helen? (Hannah's sisters)
    C: gone uh school.

9. A: what's that? (Hannah has picked up a toy duck)
    C: duck.
    A: what does a duck do?
    C: (makes pig noises)
    A: what does a duck do? quack quack.
    C: **cack cack**.
    C: (later) duck **cying**. ('crying')
    A: what? is he crying?
    C: yeah.
    A: ah. give him a love then. is he better now?
    C: yeah.
    A: (later) put your duckie to sleep on the settee.
    C: fall off. **gain** ('again'). **nat** ('that') go on.

Dialogues 10–13. Age 1;10. Hannah and Gayle are in Gayle's bedroom.

10. C: a **yittle yady**. (sees a porcelain statue of a man)
    A: a little lady?
    C: yeah.
    A: it's a man. who is it on that picture? (shows Hannah a photograph)
    C: **Dohn.**
    A: John?
    C: **Dohn.**
    A: it's not. Gayle.
    C: it's **Gay**. he got a suit on. (looking at the statue again)
    A: yeah.
    C: **dis** ('this') back up. (puts photograph on window sill)

11. A: where's the frog? (a frog figurine)
    C: **dere**.
    A: there.
    C: what's **dat** one?
    A: what's that? it's a frog.
    C: yeah. it's a **hoyabul** ('horrible') one.
    A: is it? why?
    C: it's **hoyabul** one
    A: is it naughty?
    C: yeah. naughty froggie. he nice.
    A: nice?
    C: (looks at woollen ball on the top of a toy's hat) goodie. **dat** not a **pider** ('spider')
    A: it's not a spider. it's his hat.

12. C: (sees a toy mouse) **dat** a **hoyabul** mouse.
    A: do you not like that one?
    C: (points to different objects) I **yike dat** one. I **yike dat** one. I **yike dat** one.
    A: which one? do you like that little mousie?
    C: yeah.

13. C: (hears Gayle's mother in the hall) **yat** ('that') you mum. gonna wash **bafroom**.
    A: she's going to wash the bathroom. you're a clever girl aren't you?
    C: (later) you go out. (points to bedroom door)
    A: why?
    C: go and clean you **bafroom**.

Data collected by Lucy Barker. Note that the child here is learning English with a standard American accent, and the **r** sounds in the transcriptions of the adult targets reflect this.

CORPUS VII: 2-YEAR-OLD AMERICAN GIRL

1. Age 2;2

	Adult target	Child's version
'yoghurt'	yogurt	roro
'book'	buk	bu
'puzzle'	puzl	baba
'piggy'	pigi	bibi
'tractor'	traktər	dadə
'purple'	purpl	pupə
'duck'	duk	da
'nose'	noz	nos
'ball'	bal	ba
'window'	windo	do
'stroller'	strolər	lolər
'apple'	apl	apə

2. Age 2;5

	Adult target	Child's version
'yoghurt'	yogurt	obə
'book'	buk	bu
'puzzle'	puzl	puzəl
'piggy'	pigi	pidi
'tractor'	traktər	dadər
'purple'	purpl	purpər
'duck'	duk	duk
'nose'	noz	nos
'ball'	bal	ba
'window'	windo	rido
'stroller'	strolər	lolər
'apple'	apl	apəl

ANSWERS TO FURTHER EXERCISES

Exercises are numbered by unit, therefore **Exercise 1.3** refers to the third exercise in Unit 1.

1.3

1. take = A; banana = N
2. sit = A
3. Mummy = N; give = A
4. cup = N
5. baby = N; crib = N
6. little = M
7. see = A; duck = N
8. blue = M
9. glue = N or A
10. it = N; flew = A
11. flap = N or A
12. sleep = A or possibly N
13. clock = N; ticking = A
14. slug = N; icky = M
15. Daddy = N; stick = N or A
16. big = M; nipple = N
17. got = A; asthma = N
18. handle = N
19. bus = N; little = M
20. bitten = A; me = N
21. eat = A; granola = N
22. flat = M or possibly N
23. rattle = N
24. twig = N
25. more = M; bread = N
26. smell = A or N

2.5
a. Analogical: probably based on small size.
b. Statement: *That's Mummy's coat.*
c. Categorical: extensions belong to *animal* category.
d. Categorical: extensions belong to *male human children* category.
e. Analogical: based on round shape.
f. Categorical: extensions belong to *vehicle* category.
g. Statement: *The apple's in the refrigerator* or perhaps *I want an apple from the refrigerator.*
h. Analogical: based on the common ability to float on water.

i. Analogical: based on sweetness or 'treat' aspect, although these items do belong to the very general category of food.

2.6 *wrong side* for *upside down* and *toe* for *shoe*.

2.7 a. *necklace* for *microphone*.
b. analogical based on common function: worn around the neck.

2.8 a. *Santa Claus* for *frog* and *nurse* for *stewardess*.
b. red colour and possibly texture of 'clothes'.
c. female, brings food, helps people, wears a uniform.

3.6 a. *post*
b. *put* (probably)
c. Both *post* and *put* involve causing a change of location. But the child probably has a much wider meaning for *post* than an adult. To her, it seems to mean slipping something flat through a narrow opening, just as her mother did with the counter. What the child has not learned yet is that *post* specifically refers to consigning an item to the mail service, not simply the action involved in using a post-box. Items can be *posted* in a variety of ways, including dropping them in a bag or handing them in at a desk.

3.7 **Dialogue 22**. The mother identifies the *iguana* as a *lizard* and as an *animal* (note the ascending order of generality). She could have included *reptile* which is roughly at the same level of generality as *mammal*.

3.8 a. higher
b. I'm going to the upper/higher level.
c. The more accurate opposite of *higher* (and *upper* as it is used in b.) is *lower* not *smaller* which the child uses. In the sense that *smaller* means less extension, however, its meaning is similar to *lower*. And, of course, in the case of the collapsible music stand, the result of it being lowered is that it appears smaller to the child.

4.7

1. *take*		*banana*	13. *clock*		*ticking*
verb	+	noun	noun	+	verb
action	+	affected	agent	+	action
3. *mummy*		*give*	16. *big*		*nipple*
noun	+	verb	adjective	+	noun

	agent	+	action		attribute	+	entity
6.	*me*		*little*	21.	*eat*		*granola*
	pronoun	+	adjective		verb	+	noun
	entity	+	attribute		action	+	affected

4.8 a. negation = **22**; **24** recurrence = **25** b. **4**; **5**; **15** c. **9**

4.9 a. 1a. daddy taking banana   1b. Baby   take   banana
   agent   action affected   agent action affected
   5a. Baby's   crib   5b. Baby   sleep crib
   possessor possession   agent action location
   b. 1a. Daddy; is; -ing; the 1b. can; Baby; a
   5a. see; 's 5b. Does; sleep; in; the
   c. 1a. *Daddy* content (noun); *is* function (auxiliary verb); *the* function (article).
   1b. *can* function (auxiliary verb); *Baby* content (noun); *a* function (article).
   5a. *see* content (main verb).
   5b. *Does* function (auxiliary verb); *sleep* content (main verb); *in* function (preposition); *the* function (article).

5.7 a. our   play   that.   on floor.
   agent + action + affected   location
   our   play   that   on floor.
   agent + action + affected + location
   b. *We/us* is the pronoun that refers to the speaker + someone else. Since this pronoun is in subject position its form should be *we*. Sophie is right in that *our* also refers to the speaker + someone else. But this word is only used to modify other nouns in a noun phrase, indicating the possessor: *our book*, *our problem*, etc.

5.8 a. **II:5** [1] *look*. [2] *look her toe*.
   b. [1] action. [2] action + location/direction. Within location/direction is possessor + possession.
   c. preposition *at* omitted.

5.9 a. **II:9** all those children. me playing all those children.
   b. Preposition *with* omitted.

6.9 ***2.** I   I = insert negative inside sentence
    7. O   O = place negative outside basic sentence
    *8. I   * = conforms to Stage II rules
   *10. I
   *11. I
   12. O
   18. O
   19. O
   22. O

6.10 **I:2** = rejection; **I:8** = denial; **I:12** = rejection;
I:18 = non-existence; **II:3** = denial;
II:18 = denial; **II:19** = non-existence; **III:2** = denial;
III:4 = rejection; **III:5** = rejection; **V:13** = rejection.

6.11

Sophie	*Alison*	*Kathryn*
d'*	may	'm (am)
would × 3	'll (will) × 2	won't
don't	can	'll × 2
won't		can
can × 2		
's (has)		

* Might she be fudging the *do/did* issue here?

6.12 **2.** past marked on both auxiliary and main verb.
   9. double negative.
  14. order of auxiliary and subject not reversed.

6.13 **II:17** *hear* what; *think* what

7.6 a. You may have others . . . *baker* (someone who bakes);
runner (someone who runs); *killer* (someone who kills)
  b. **4.** *typewriter* and **15.** *puncher*.
  c. *typewriter*. In English, this word means only the *instrument* involved in typewriting not the *agent*.
  d. **15.** *badder*. In English, -*er* can also be added to many words (usually adjectives) to mean *more* as in *green/greener* or *silly/sillier*. The child has overgeneralized the use of the suffix in this case since *more bad* in English requires an irregular form *worse*. In **II:20**, Sophie might have coined *upper* on the spur of the moment with the sense of *I want it to go up more*.

7.7   a. **10. conversion** of a noun *broom* to a verb meaning *to use a broom*.

  14. conversion of a noun *jam* to a verb meaning *to put jam on something*.

b. You may have others:

  10. noun *hammer* to verb *to hammer* (a nail).

  noun *knife* to verb *to knife* (someone).

  noun *spoon* to verb *to spoon* (the sauce).

  14. noun *butter* to verb *to butter* (bread).

  noun *salt* to verb *to salt* (the gravy).

  noun *water* to verb *to water* (the lawn).

c. *to use a broom* (**10.**) = *to sweep*.

7.8   Adding the suffix *-y* to a noun, can form an adjective meaning similar to the noun or characterized by the noun. Examples: Noun – *mud* Adjective – *muddy*; Noun – *dirt* Adjective – *dirty*; Noun – *salt* Adjective – *salty*

7.9   **II:22** *he's face* for *his face*. The rule for indicating possession in a noun phrase is to add a suffix to the word or phrase referring to the possessor: ***Annie's*** *ball*, **the dog's** *collar*. In writing, this appears as *'s*, but in spoken language, this suffix shows the same **s/z/iz** sound alternations as the *-s* added to plural nouns. However, when we want to refer to the possessor with a pro-form, special possessive forms are used: *his, her, my, our, your, their*.

7.10   a. The sense here is *It bit me*. In some circumstances, much older children and adults could have used *It has bitten me*. This is another way of expressing past events. Notice that irregular verbs in English often have two forms depending on the construction:

  *I **was** /I have **been*** or *I **forgot** /I have **forgotten**.*

In this case the child has used the verb form from the *have* construction.

b. Notice how often **Sophie** uses verb forms of this type when talking about past events, often without *have*.

8.1   *you are taking a bissy* (ongoing); *you took a bissy* (past); *you can take a bissy* (possibility). Mother chooses past: *'cause I **was** hungry*.

8.2 a. **3.** adds *-ing* to *come* and *-ing* to *find*.
  7. adds *-ed* to *step*.
  9. removes *-s* from *childrens*.
  b. **10.** *'ve* (have got) **16.** *have* (have forgotten) **24.** *have* (have got).

8.3 a. *me want* + action or object.
  b. **20.** *Why d'you never* **buy me a guitar**? *Can you* **make it go upper**?
  21. *Shall we go to Barnett's?* This is very subtle – she obviously wants mother to buy her sweets.
  23. *Can you* **read it**? (Compare to **II:5**)
  24. *Can we have some cucumber for lunch?* Again quite a subtle approach, considering what she wants the cucumber for.
  c. *Why don't you shut your*—**shut your door?**

8.4 **II:2** I didn't put biscuit on there. (needs *a* or *the*)
  II:3 finding her cheque-book. (uses *her* for *his* and *find* for *look*)
  II:22 **guanas**. (uses child's pronunciation of *iguana*)

9.7 a. (piano) *pyano:pano* **y** deleted; (biscuit) *biskit:bisi* **k** deleted.
  b. **pl**ay, **fl**oor, **br**oke, **st**ep, hel**p**.

9.8 a. *handl:handu*; *litl:litu*; *bitn:bitu*. Substitution of vowel sound **u** for syllabic consonants **l** and **n**.
  b. *kotn:kotu*; *botl:botu*.

9.9 a. *bissy* and *blanky*. Final t deleted.
  b. *seen* (plasticine); *gotten* (forgotten);
  nother (another); *guana* (iguana);
  corder (recorder): *cuz* (because).

9.10 **21.** a. *granola:ola*; b. CCVCVCV:VCV; c. syllable deletion.
  22. a. *flat:fat*; b. CCVC:CVC; c. consonant cluster reduction.
  23. a. *ratl:ratu*; b. CVCC:CVCV c. vowel replaces syllabic consonant.
  24. a. *twig:ti* b. CCVC:CV c. cluster reduction and final consonant deletion.
  25. a. *bred:bəred* b. CCVC:CVCVC c. vowel addition to split consonant cluster.

26. a. *smel:melə* b. CCVC:CVCV c. cluster reduction and final vowel addition.

9.11 a. 1. Cluster reduction (**sk** to **k**) and final consonant deletion (**t**).
  2. Cluster reduction (**st** to **t**) and final consonant deletion (**k**).
  3. Addition of vowel to avoid word-final consonant sound.
  4. Final consonant deletion (**k**).
  5. Syllable deletion (**ko**).
  6. Cluster reduction (**kw** to **p**). Notice that a completely different consonant has replaced the cluster.

  b. 1. CVCCVC:CVCV   4. CVCVC:CVCV
  2. CCVCVC:CVCV   5. CVCVCV:CVCV
  3. CVC:CVCV   6. CCVCV:CVCV

  All the baby versions consist of simple alternations of consonants and vowels and, with the exception of **3.**, all baby versions contain fewer individual sounds.

10.5 a. *kik/gik; flap/vlap; kod/got; hav/haf; toi/doi.*
  Child uses a voiced consonant for the initial consonant and a voiceless one for the final consonant in a word. Note that the place and manner of articulation of the target consonants remains the same.

  b. *pig* to *bik*; *keep* to *geep*; *bit* to *bit*.

10.6 a. *banana* = partial assimilation to later nasal consonant **n** (**b** to **m**).
  sit = stopping (**s** to **t**).
  giv = stopping (**v** to **b**).
  kup = initial consonant voicing (**k** to **g**).
  krib = final consonant de-voicing (**b** to **p**).
  litl = reduplication of first syllable
  duk = partial assimilation to later velar consonant **k** (**d** to **g**).

  b. *buz* to *bud*; *top* to *dop*.

10.7 a. *blu/bu; glu/gu; flu/lu; flap/lap; sleep/leep; klok/kok; slug/lug.*
  All are cases of consonant cluster reduction by consonant deletion.

  b. In consonant clusters containing **l** as the second consonant, the child deletes the **l** if the initial consonant is a stop but deletes the initial consonant if it is a fricative.

10.8 *on* to *mon*. The nasal quality of the **n** probably had an influence here. Could she have been thinking of *upon*? Notice that both **p** and **m** are labials.

10.9 *gangan* for *grandmother*. Involves consonant cluster reduction (**gr** to **g**); deletion of final **d** in first syllable; reduplication of first syllable.

10.10 (stick) Target = *stik* Child = *kik*
1. consonant cluster reduction (**st** to **t**).
2. assimilation to later velar consonant (**t** to **k**).

(nipple) Target = *nipl* Child = *mipu*
1. partial assimilation to later labial consonant **p** (**n** to **m**).
2. replacement of syllabic consonant by vowel (**l** to **u**).

(asthma) Target = asmə Child = apmə
1. stopping (**s** to **t**).
2. partial assimilation to later labial consonant **m** (**t** to **p**).

INDEX OF KEY WORDS AND TECHNICAL TERMS

The page numbers in **bold** indicate where a KEY WORD is defined and/or illustrated by examples. Authors' names which appear in this index are those specifically mentioned in the text or exercises for Units 1–12 (*see also* Further Reading).